ENGLISH ESSAYS FROM A FRENCH PEN

Cy commencent les chapitres de phē filz
faint loys. Le pꝛmier Oune bataille ꝗ

FRENCH SHIPS, OF THE EARLY PART OF THE XVᵀᴴ CENTURY,
ILLUSTRATIVE OF REGNAULT GIRARD'S JOURNEY.

Walter L.Colls,Ph.Sc.

ENGLISH ESSAYS

FROM

A FRENCH PEN

BY

J. J. JUSSERAND

AMS PRESS
NEW YORK

Reprinted from the edition of 1895, London
First AMS EDITION published 1970
Manufactured in the United States of America

Library of Congress Catalog Card Number: 77-112488
SBN: 404-03624-4

AMS PRESS, INC.
NEW YORK, N.Y. 10003

I have to present my best thanks to Mr. James Knowles and to Messrs. Lawrence and Bullen, who very kindly authorize me to reprint the " Journeys" to Scotland and to England, first published in the " Nineteenth Century," and the essay on Paul Scarron, printed as an introduction to " The Comical Romance and other tales, illustrated from the designs of Oudry" (Lawrence and Bullen, 1892).

J.

June 9, 1895.

CONTENTS

LIST OF ILLUSTRATIONS

English Essays from a French Pen.

———•◇•———

I.

THE FORBIDDEN PASTIMES OF A RECLUSE.

(England—Twelfth Century.)

ETHELRED, Ailred, or Aeldred, sometime Abbot of Rievaulx, then one of the most important monasteries and now one of the finest ruins in England, was born at Hexham about 1109. He was brought up at the court of David, king of Scotland, the founder of Melrose and Holyrood, and was the companion of Henry, son of that king. He was appointed Abbot of Rievaulx in 1146, and died twenty years later, famous for his piety, his wisdom, and his religious zeal, no less than for his learning and his

works.   He left a great many writings on historical
or theological subjects, all of them in Latin.   He was
canonised in 1191, and his feast is on the 12th of
January.

He had a sister, sister in the flesh and in the
spirit, " carne et spiritu," says he, whom he dearly
loved, and who, following examples not very rare
in those troubled times, had become an anchoress
or recluse.   Recluses and hermits were numerous ;
they assigned to themselves strict duties, and pledged
themselves to the practising of very severe austerities,
the hardest of these being their total separation from
the outside world.   Not a few discovered, when the
great resolve had been taken, that the Tempter was
not to be met only in public places and in merry
gatherings : he found his way into the best-immured
cells, and knocked at the gate of the heart.   And the
gate of the heart sometimes opened, and the life of
austerities came to an end.   It had begun as a canticle,
and ended as a fabliau.

This juxtaposition of contraries is of constant occurrence in the Middle Ages ; opposite extremes are drawn
to each other and meet.   The wealthiest convents
belong to friars who have made a vow of poverty ; mad
songs and pious songs are sung at Christmas to the
same tunes : songs so holy that they seem to come

from heaven, and songs so revolting that a certain
notable man, according to Gascoigne, died of shame
at the mere remembrance of them. Anchoresses flee
from the world, and settle, each one by herself, in a
cell, there to think only of God and of their salvation.
In those quiet retreats, far from the multitude, sheltered
from the noise of the great world, dead as it seems to
the joys of life, recluses, instead of finding rest, found
trouble. Mundane thoughts could not be walled out;
unedifying stories recurred to their mind, and filled it
with indecent images; in their peaceful fortresses they
had to undergo sieges; the world might be ignorant
of the fact, but their confessor knew it. The unfortu-
nate recluses were besieged by Love.

To this testifies Aelred, Abbot of Rievaulx. He
himself never led the life of a recluse; he is sorry for
it, because he would otherwise be in a better position
to give useful counsel, and others would be able to
profit by his experience.[1] But he has at least observed
the people about him; and so, while deriving from
St. Benedict most of the advice he gives concerning food, raiment, fasting, &c., he adds, "some
things meant especially for this time and country";
pro loco et tempore quædam. In these "things" lies

---

[1] "Utinam a sapientiore id peteres et impetrares : qui non con-
jectura qualibet sed experientia didicisset quod alios doceret."

the main interest of his " Rule for Recluses, written for his sister " ; [1] a work not often read to-day, but which deserves to be better known, as it affords a most curious illustration of the manners of that remote period.

It is, says he, a very good thing to shut one's self up, like the hermits of old who lived in the desert, or like those who, impelled by a pious zeal, cause themselves to be immured in their cells. But to shut the body in is nothing ; the danger will continue great, even for the body, if the soul wanders, and if, " owing to vain talk, the mind journeys towards the towns, amongst the streets, to fairs and places where people are gathered together."

A breach exists in the anchoresses' holy citadel ; the door is closed, or even walled up ; but there remains the window. This is the weak point ; and through it the foe will get in. He will enter under various disguises ; illegitimate thoughts will creep in, laughable tales will be told ; at times also the enemy will take less immaterial shapes. The window is the cause of the main anxieties felt by the authors of rules for

[1] " Regula sive Institutio Inclusarum, ad sororem."—" Lucæ Holstenii . . . Codex Regularum monasticarum." Augusti Vindelicorum, 1759, fol., vol. vi. p. 420. The oldest MS. of the " Regula " preserved in the British Museum is the MS. Cotton Nero, A. iii.

recluses. An opening doubtless was needed to let day-
light in, and in the case of an immured cell food also.
But what a dangerous need ! Most of the evil that
happens is to be traced to the window. In the famous
Ancren Riwle,[1] drawn up in the following (thirteenth)
century, the " caveats " are as numerous and pressing
as they are here. " My dear master," a recluse is
supposed to say to the author of the *Riwle*, " is it now
so very evil a thing to look out ? "

" Yea it is, dear sister, for the harm that comes of it
is evil above evil to every anchorite, and especially to
the young. . . . If any one reprove them, then they
immediately say : ' Sir, she does the same who is better
than I am, and knows better what she ought to do.'
O dear young recluse, often does a right skilful smith
forge a full weak knife ; the wise ought to imitate
wisdom, not folly."

The same anxieties are displayed by Abbot Aelred.
The recluse, as he describes her, sits at her window, and
through the window, busy and inventive as a prisoner,
she manages to arrange for herself a sort of active life ;
she follows worldly interests ; she wants to escape
the monotony of protracted meditations and long
prayers. There are recluses who by means of their

[1] " The Ancren Riwle," ed. J. Morton, London, Camden
Society, 1853, 4to, p. 53.

window addict themselves to the tilling of the land or the keeping of a herd, and who give so much attention to the cultivation of the fields around them that you would take them for ladies, not for anchoresses.[1]

Others call children together, and while away the time by keeping a school ; the children sit under the porch, and the recluse teaches them from her window : " Illa sedet ad fenestram, istæ in porticu resident." She encourages, rewards, punishes them, and on occasion—poor secluded woman—covers them with kisses, calling a little one who weeps " her daughter, her friend." [2]

Sometimes—Aelred even says " often "—the occupations are of a much lighter and more objectionable kind. Before the window, always the window, an old woman " vetula " is sitting, and she assigns to herself the task of entertaining the recluse. She tells her the last scandal of the town, the newest gossip ; she gives an account of the mad pranks of young libertines ; she tells her some of those merry tales which are the

---

[1] " . . . Vel multiplicandis pecoribus inhiant : tantaque sollicitudine in his extenduntur ut eas matres vel dominas familiarum æstimes, non anachoretas."

[2] " Nunc ridet nunc minatur, nunc percutit, nunc blanditur, nunc osculatur, nunc flentem vocat pro verbere propius, palpat faciem, stringit collum, et in amplexum ruens, nunc filiam vocat, nunc amicam."

groundwork of fabliaux. Were her stories in verse, they would in fact be real fabliaux. The case is not an isolated one ; the same thing happens, the same garrulous old woman is to be observed, " with nearly all the recluses of our time." Stories are thus circulated of dissolute monks, wanton girls, and wronged husbands. Most of the typical heroes of the *Decamerone* are called up by Aelred long before their day, and we gather from the account he supplies of those talks under the window that the stories were as complete as Boccaccio's. The old woman would give descriptions of the personages, details concerning their outward appearance, their features, their manners and their ways ; also full particulars about the tricks resorted to by wives to deceive their friends or husbands.[1] There can be no doubt as to the nature of those tales : except for the verse they are fabliaux, that is laughable tales ;[2] for Aelred adds : " The lips thereupon are shaken

---

[1] " Vix aliquam inclusarum hujus temporis solam invenies, ante cujus fenestram non anus garrula vel nugigerula mulier sedeat, quæ eam fabulis occupet, rumoribus aut detractionibus pascat, illius vel illius monaci vel clerici vel alterius cujuslibet ordinis viri formam, vultum moresque describat. Illecebrosa quoque interserat, puellarum lasciviam, viduarum, quibus licet quidquid libet, conjugum in viris fallendis explendisque voluptatibus astutiam depingat."

[2] " Les Fabliaux sont des contes à rire, en vers." Bédier, " Les Fabliaux," 1893, p. 6.

2

with laughter, and the sweet poison, once drunk, pervades the heart and the whole body."

Those old story-telling women are very dangerous ; recluses are never tired of listening to them ; and they give them, as a reward, all they can, and share their food with them.   Left alone, at dusk, they suffer no longer from their solitude ; the image of the heroes of those amusing tales has remained in their minds, and keeps them company ; the long hours have become short ; they are "inebriated" by such sweet remembrances, and now " they go wrong while singing their psalms and have falls while reading the day's lessons."

What, then, is the ultimate result of those talks, the memory of which so completely fills the mind, and which run on things so pleasant, it seems, to remember, but so ugly in truth to look at ?   The result is that the listener sometimes assumes a less passive rôle ; she first liked to hear, and now she likes to imitate ; she will soon become herself a fit subject for a tale or a fabliau.   She thinks, she contrives ; assignations are made, and the pure cell meant for a holy life is transformed into a place of debauchery.[1]

---

[1]   "Nam manifestior sermo non jam de accendenda, sed potius de satianda voluptate procedens, ubi et quando et per quem possit explere quod cogitat, in commune exponunt.   Cella utitur in prostibulum, et delicato qualibet arte, foramine, aut illa egreditur, aut adulter ingreditur."

Thus the recluse in her turn supplies the authors of fabliaux with plots for which they will not, this time, have to look beyond the mountains and the seas. They will only have to open their eyes and ears, and note what takes place around them. If a small number among the popular tales of the Middle Ages come from India, a much larger proportion are made out of real life, true events, traits of character, which it was possible for the observer to note in many countries during that period. The holy Abbot of Rievaulx relates himself, by way of example and admonition, one or two knaves' tricks, drawn from life, which have been the subject of many licentious fabliaux ; standard tricks, if one may say so, which are to be found in every collection of tales. The very title of one of the chapters of his " Rule for Recluses " might indeed be taken for the title of a chapter in the *Decamerone*.[1]

What must be done therefore in a time when the religious rules are so hard, and physical passions so vehement ? Aelred does not hesitate : the rules must be made harder ; all communication, all contact, every worldly sight is to be avoided. Beware of every man, even of your confessor ; do not take pleasure in seeing him too often ; do not fail to choose him as old as

---

[1] " Contra illos qui dicunt se esse frigidos, vel impotentes, et in lecto se cum mulieribus ponunt, duplex malum cumulantes."

possible ; be careful never to allow him to play with your hand : " Nec ipsi manum suam tangendam præbeat vel palpandam."

Younger men must of course be avoided with even greater care ; for it is much more difficult, the holy Abbot says, to resist them. Mind you do not accept from some young man, " under pretence of spiritual amity, letters or little gifts." [1] Do not embroider for him, " as is done so often," purses or girdles in threads of various colours. All this serves no purpose, " but to foment unlawful love, and cause great sins." For no doubt is possible, the fortress is besieged, and Love is the besieger.

One cannot be too much on guard against Love. On account of him many sorts of good works will have to be discarded. Helping the poor, sheltering the traveller, are works of mercy ; yet the recluse will abstain from them. A very difficult rule, the recluse will perhaps say ; what can I do to prevent "clamouring poor, weeping orphans, crying widows from gathering round my cell ? " How can their coming be avoided ?

---

[1] " Adolescentium et suspectarum personarum devita colloquium . . . Nunquam inter te et quemlibet virum, quasi occasione exhibendæ charitatis vel nutriendi affectus, vel expetendæ familiaritatis aut amicitiæ spiritualis, discurrant nuntii ; nec eorum munuscula literasque suscipias, nec illis tua dirigas, prout moris est, puta zonas, marsupia, quæ diverso stamine variata sunt."

For the poor flock there, and they give vent more freely to their noisy supplications as they stand under the window of a woman who is godly, and who, besides, cannot move away. Never mind, the abbot answers, "be seated, keep silent, let them alone; they will at length perceive that you have nothing, and can give nothing; they will get tired and desist." [1] To fortify herself against the temptation to be charitable, the recluse will live only upon the produce of her own work; or, if that is not possible, she must, before she is shut in, make arrangements with trusty people, "in order that there may be brought to her each day exactly what she wants for a day." [2]

Those herds of beggars are more dangerous than they seem; and here again Aelred sketches a little scene worthy of a fabliau or of the *Decamerone*. In the midst of those beggars, cripples and wretches, the same enemy, the great and sweet enemy, Love, finds

---

[1] "Non circa cellulam ejus pauperes clament, non orphani plorent, non vidua lementetur. Sed quis, inquies, hoc poterit prohibere ?—Tu sede, tu tace, tu sustine; mox ut scient te nihil habere, seque nihil recepturos, vel fatigati discedent."

[2] "Quod reclusa de proprio labore vivat . . . Si autem aut infirmitas, aut teneritudo non permittat, antequam includatur, certas personas quærat, a quibus singulis diebus quod uni diei sufficiat, humiliter recipiat; nec causa pauperum vel hospitium quidquam adjiciat. . . . Magnæ infidelitatis signum est si inclusa de crastino sit sollicita."

his way.   Unobserved in the group of the poor, some
perfidious woman, a tempter, " insidiatrix pudicitiæ,"
will come quite close and speak to you in favour of a
monk or a clerk, and drop melting words, " blanda
verba," into your ear.   Your alms will be the pretext
and the means ; she will come quite close to kiss
your hand, under pretence of gratitude.

Hospitality is much less to be recommended to a
wise recluse, even that rough sort of hospitality which
a recluse could give, and which consisted in allowing
some women to sleep under the shelter or porch before
her window : " ante inclusæ fenestram discumbentes."
For in such cases, no one sleeps ; neither the recluse
nor her guests, among whom will often be found women
of the worst kind, " pessimæ," who will not talk much
about religion, you may be sure, but " about love " ;
and almost the whole of the night will be thus spent
without sleep.[1]   Under the window of the recluse, all
the night long, Love keeps watch.

---

[1] " Cavendum præterea est, ut nec ob susceptionem religiosarum
fœminarum quodlibet hospitalitatis onus inclusa suscipiat.   Nam
inter bonas plerumque etiam pessimæ veniunt, quæ ante inclusæ
fenestram discumbentes præmissis valde paucis de religiosis ser-
monibus ad sæcularia devolvuntur, inde subtexere amatoria, et
noctem fere totam insomnem ducere.   Sane tu tales devita, ne
cogaris audire, quod videre horreas ; forte enim videbuntur amara
cùm audiuntur vel cernuntur, quæ sequuntur dulcia cùm cogi-
tantur."

The World must be shut out; the cell must be bare : "the walls must not be hung, nor covered with various paintings." [1] In the case of absolute necessity, and this is in truth a very notable concession, the recluse will be allowed the help of a matron to whom her relations with the outside will be entrusted, and of a serving maid, who will carry the wood and water, and bake the peas and vegetables. But it must be understood that each of the two shall be perfect of her kind ; neither talkative, nor quarrelsome, nor addicted to tale-telling. The maid especially must be closely watched for fear, lest by means of her, the Fiend should get access to the house : " Ne forte ejus lascivia tuum sanctum habitaculum polluatur."

Thus did the holy Abbot of Rievaulx show the way to heaven to his dearly beloved sister, allowing her to profit by his own observations (as he is careful to note here and there : "I knew a certain monk. . . ." "I saw a man . . .") ; and thus he taught her by what hard means and cruel sacrifices a life of quiet, pleasing to God, could be led, in the stormy days when King Henry the Second reigned over England.

[1] " Est etiam quædam species vanitatis in affectata aliqua pulchritudine etiam intra cellulam delectari, parietes variis picturis et celaturis ornare, oratorium pannorum et imaginum varietate decorare. Hæc omnia, quasi professioni tuæ contraria, cave."

II.

A JOURNEY TO SCOTLAND IN THE YEAR 1435.

I.—Regnault Girard.

A JOURNEY to Scotland was not, in the fifteenth century, the pleasure trip so many tourists have since accomplished. It was a serious and difficult undertaking, not to be attempted lightly. The men from abroad who visited the kingdom in those times usually came on important business ; they came, in fact, because they could not do otherwise ; salmon and grouse were not considered then a sufficient attraction ; no hotels had been built in picturesque spots, the beauties of Loch Lomond and Loch Katrine were allowed to pass unobserved and unvisited.

The country was so far distant, so secluded from the rest of the world, that rather vague notions were entertained as to its very situation. We have an account of the kingdom, written in the year 1498, in which it is described as " bordering by sea on Brittany, France, and Flanders. Towards the west there is no land between Scotland and Spain. Scotland is nearer to Spain than London."[1] Strange as it may seem, these geographical particulars are not supplied by some ignorant compiler writing from hearsay, but by no less a person than Don Pedro de Ayala, Spanish ambassador at the Scottish Court. He had drawn up his report at the particular request and for the enlightenment of his masters, Ferdinand and Isabella, " who desired a full description of Scotland and its king."

Near to France and Spain as the country was supposed to be, according to ambassadorial observation, still experience proved that the journey was not a short one. Tempests were frequent, much more indeed than now, for the reason that what we call a rough sea was a storm for the quaint unmanageable ships of the period. The sea, besides, was held by the English—a fact which contributed in no slight degree to diminish the enjoyment of journeys between Scotland and the Continent. The actual ruler of the country, King James the First, was a living example of what could be

[1] " Early Travellers in Scotland," ed. P. Hume Brown, Edinb., 1891, 8vo, p. 48.

expected, as he had been taken by the English in his youth, when on his way to France, and had remained nineteen years a captive in the Tower of London, at Newark, Evesham, and in other prisons.

When the sea was smooth, and the English were busy elsewhere, then the traveller had to fight another enemy, namely *ennui :* he had no comfortable accommodation in which to sleep away the time, no novels to read, no tobacco to smoke ; the numerous days he was bound to spend in his ship appeared even more numerous. Froissart has given us a description of those long tiresome journeys, and the means resorted to in order to fill the empty hours : passengers played dice, or made bets ; a knight laid a wager that he would climb in full armour to the top of the mast; while performing the deed his foot slipped, he fell into the sea, and the weight of his armour sank him in a moment. " All the barons were much vexed at this misfortune," observes Froissart by way of funeral oration, " but they were forced to endure it, as they could not in any way remedy it."

Tiresome or dangerous as they were, still journeys had to be undertaken. Scotland played then a part of its own in European politics ; she fought the English not only on the Border, but also by the Loire, with her auld ally, France. Intercourse had to be kept up.

Ambassadors came from the French or Spanish king, from the Pope, from the fathers of the Basle Council. Several of them took care to leave an account of their experience of far-off Scotland, and their journals have been recently collected by Mr. P. Hume Brown under the title "Early Travellers in Scotland." There will be found descriptions of the kingdom by Jean Froissart, Æneas Sylvius Piccolomini, who was to be Pope Pius the Second, George Chastelain, Pedro de Ayala, and others. This fine collection is not however quite complete, and one at least very curious document has escaped the notice of the learned editor.

This document consists in the report drawn by the French ambassador sent to Scotland in the years 1434–6 by King Charles the Seventh, to fetch the Lady Margaret, daughter of James the First, who had been betrothed six years before to Louis, Dauphin de Viennois, heir to the crown and the future Louis the Eleventh. This "Relation" remains unprinted to this day ; it is in French, and is preserved in the National Library, Paris.[1]

Everybody knows how King Charles of France, who was not yet Charles le Victorieux, and had not been rescued by Jeanne d'Arc, wanting to tighten the bonds

[1] MS. Français 17330. An edition is being prepared by Mr. Andrew Lang for the Roxburghe Club.

between his and the Scottish kingdom, had despatched in 1427 a mission to King James, asking for the hand of his daughter Margaret.   The mission was composed of John Stuart of Darnley, " constable of the Scotch in France," of Regnault de Chartres, archbishop-duke of Reims, and of Alain Chartier the poet, to whom the oratorical part of the business had been entrusted. Alain delivered in the presence of the king, queen, and assembled Court such a beautiful Latin speech that it made matters quite easy for the other ambassadors. The speech has come down to us, and a copy of it is preserved at Paris.   But, as the betrothed was only three years old, and the dauphin five, the two royal families considered that the marriage could be conveniently postponed, and it was only when the couple had reached riper years, being then nine and eleven respectively, that the French king decided to send for the dauphiness that was to be.

His choice for this important mission fell upon Maître Regnault Girard, knight, Seigneur de Bazoges, one of his councillors and masters of the hostel ; a very worthy man indeed, prudent, trusty, and wise, but as little warlike and as little inclined to seamanship as he well could be.   The news of the great honour bestowed upon his person was to him most unwelcome ; the idea of the turbulent sea and hostile English was too much for his pacific mind ; he was, indeed, unable to bear it. Honest Regnault Girard, knight, forgetting entirely his knighthood, bethought himself of some means to eschew the unattractive duty, and resorted to one which would be considered very strange in our day. He made it known that he would pay down the sum of 400 crowns to the plucky one who would consent to be ambassador in his stead.

But even then the thing was considered inconsistent with the discipline to be maintained in a kingdom. Charles informed his councillor and master of the hostel that he had to go in his own person to Scotland, and in order to be fully assured that the Seigneur de Bazoges would not escape, he sent the Comte de Vendosme to La Rochelle to see the unwilling ambassador off. Regnault Girard had therefore no choice ; he had no shame nor remorse either, for if he was not plucky he was honest, and we have the story of the 400 crowns on his own testimony. He has noted it in his " Relation," as a proof doubtless, if not of his courage, at least of his wisdom and foresight. " I did not like in the least to go," says he, not only on account of the season, " but also because the king was at war with the King of England and the Duke of Burgundy, and could not expect any help from the Bretons. For which cause the said embassy was a full perilous and dangerous one, and to avoid the danger of the sea I offered 400 crowns to the one who would undertake the journey, so that the king would hold me excused. But the king would never consent, and ordered me expressly to go, . . . for I was meant to obey him, as he was my master and sovereign lord."

II.—THE JOURNEY.

With a sorrowful heart and painful misgivings, the ambassador got ready and took his way towards the sea. He was accompanied by his son Joachim ; this one, at least, had no fear, either of the sea, the English, or anything. Others came, too, who were also to be of the journey, among them a famous lawyer, " famosus clericus," says Bower, Aymeri Martineau by name, who would be of use to draw up deeds and ducuments ; and also a man who was to prove very useful in his way, called Candé, or Crenedé in Girard's " Relation," Hugh Kennedy of his true name, a sturdy Scotchman, who had " fait ses preuves " at Beaugé by the side of La Hire, and who, unlike the ambassador, enjoyed the idea of the expedition very much.

Monseigneur de Vendosme did not fail in his duty, and met the travellers at La Rochelle, one of the few ports belonging then to the French Crown. He had

with him instructions made out at Orleans and signed
by the king, containing a lengthy account of what the
ambassador would have to say ; also the agreement
between Charles on the one hand and J. Puver on the
other, the latter undertaking to provide the " navy "
necessary for the bringing home of the dauphiness,
with an escort of about two thousand Scotchmen.
Puver was to feed them on board and the king was to
pay him five reals a head—that is 6,000 reals at the
beginning of the journey, and the remainder on his
return.   Then follow some provisoes which we may
suppose made poor Regnault Girard shudder : the king
stated what he would do in the case of Puver's " navy "
being rifled by the English, and in the case of Puver
himself being taken.   If the mishap occurred to the
" navy " during the outward journey, Puver would
receive nothing beyond what would have been paid
to him at starting ; if it occurred during the homeward journey then a full payment would be due.   In
case of his being taken, the king " will help him to the
value of 400 reals."   The whole being promised by
the prince " in good faith, and upon his word as a
king."

These papers and some others having been given to
Regnault Girard, who copies them in full in his " Relation," Vendosme informed him that Charles had taken

care to fix the particular day on which they were to sail, namely, the 14th of November, 1434. They all, therefore, got ready, and at the appointed time the embassy left the town to go to what was then the usual starting-place, the little hamlet of Chef-de-Baye, on the sea, one league from La Rochelle. They were accompanied by Vendosme and by the good men of the city on horseback, to the number of one hundred or more. " We then took leave to go on board, which was not without great sorrow and tears on both sides. Then we went into a boat, which took us to a whaler belonging to me Regnault Girard, of which whaler the master was (after God) Tassin Petel. We numbered altogether sixty-three persons, including seamen as well as land men. Puver was of the journey, and came in his own ship, which was well filled with goods."

All went well at first. The travellers had put to sea " with God's blessing " on the evening of the 14th, and four days later, on the 18th of November, towards two in the morning, they found themselves off the Scilly Islands. But there their troubles began, and their worst anticipations were fulfilled. " There, on the sudden, we were caught by such a great and marvellous storm, that we missed the harbour in the said islands. We missed the land of Ireland, and we had, according to the advice of the sailors, to launch into the great ocean sea. And the said tempest lasted for five days and five nights; we were driven more than a hundred leagues beyond Ireland, according to the chart. The storm was so great that we were divided from Puver's ship, and lost sight of her."

The unwilling navigator and envoy was in fact, and unknown to him, on his way to America. But this unexpected glory was not reserved for him, and he was not to discover the other shore of the "great ocean sea." He made a vow to an Irish saint whom he calls "St. Treigney" (St. Trenan), who was supposed to enjoy great influence in heaven, and who had then a greater fame on earth than he has now; for which reason, it will not be perhaps useless to point out how well chosen the saint was to whom Girard applied in this pressing necessity. Trenan was a monk of the sixth century, and a disciple of St. Columba; he had had once to undertake, by order of his chief, a journey between Ireland and Scotland; at the appointed time, the pilot who was to guide his ship was not to be found, and Trenan inclined, therefore, not to go; but Columba, addressing him, said: " Go all the same; thou wilt find wind and weather as thou wishest." Trenan put to sea, the winds filled his sails, and it seemed as if they were guiding the ship themselves;

and the monk reached happily and miraculously the opposite shore.

Regnault Girard remembered this in good time, and promised the blessed navigator a silver ship, to be hung from the roof of his chapel in Wales, with the arms of France engraved on it. Not in vain. The tempest abated, and the sailors were again able to steer their boat. They made anew for Ireland, "and on the 24th day of the same month of November, by the grace of God, we reached the extreme end of Ireland, and there found a very high and marvellous rock called Ribon, which stands at the very end of all lands, towards the west. It is an uninhabitable land ; and there we anchored under the shelter of this rock. But then the tempest began again, and for five days we had to fight the storm ; and our anchors and ropes sustained great damage."

On the 29th they left their place of shelter, and, while the sea continued very rough, they "risked the adventure," and followed the Irish coast, though none of their seamen had ever been there, and the land was an unknown and a desert one. At length, on the second day of December, they perceived that the land was no longer so wild ; habitations were descried, and they began again to know where they were. They sailed past " St. Patrick," then past " Le rax de Cantier "—

that is, the Mull of Cantire, a "marvellous place," situated "between Ireland and the wild islands of Scotland." They had then an additional satisfaction, for they met the long-lost Puver, with his ship, quite safe.

At last, on the 8th of January, 1435, they found themselves once more on dry ground, and they landed in Scotland, " having remained at sea from the 14th of November, when we left La Rochelle, for fifty-six days together, in the very heart of winter, and in stormy weather. And we had a great deal to endure, we ran great risks, and experienced adventures which it would be too long to tell."

III.—THE STAY IN SCOTLAND.

On Scotch ground Kennedy became a most useful associate; a true Scotchman, he proved to be hospitable, clever, and practical. The first thing he did was to make his companions enjoy the benefit of clanship and kinship. He took his worn-out fellow-travellers to the house or "hostel" of a lady to whom he was related, the house being called "Hostel Cambel." The lady received them very well, and made them good cheer, the more willingly as a son of hers, as was the case then in many Scotch families, "had served the King of France as body-guard."

Thoroughly refreshed and comforted, the travellers remembered " St. Treigney," and, before beginning their land journey towards Edinburgh, they made their pilgrimage and offered to their protector, as agreed, a silver ship bearing the arms of France. They had in the meanwhile despatched a messenger towards King James, to inform him of their coming and ask to be admitted to his presence. On the 14th of January, their pilgrimage being ended, they were again in the friendly house of Kennedy, " who feasted us greatly. He had called to meet us a number of his friends and relations. Then we went to Dompbertrain (Dumbarton) [1] and there remained six days waiting for the answer of the King of Scotland." While there, they learnt, with no little anxiety, that a brother of the Scotch queen (Jane Beaufort, granddaughter of John of Gaunt), " brother also of the Earl of Somerset in England, had come to Scotland in great state with a mission to prevent the intended marriage of our lord the dauphin."

In consideration of this news, Kennedy observed that, after all the splendour displayed by the English envoy,

---

[1] " C'est un fort des plus munis qu'il y ait dans toute l'Escosse et à cause de sa situation et de sa nature. Car il est situé tout proche les confluences des fleuves dans une plaine herbeuse et comme attaché à un rocher aspre et roide." Jean de Blaev, " Le Théâtre du Monde," Amsterdam, 1654, fol. vol. vi. p. 87.

it would be unwise and contrary to the dignity of the French king if his ambassadors made their entry into Edinburgh, "which is the chief town of Scotland," without having a proper retinue and escort. He therefore called together as many as he could of his relations and friends ; they came on horseback, knights all of them, or esquires, and the French embassy was thus enabled to make some figure, as they were sixty horse altogether when entering the town. To honour them, the king had sent to meet them on their way the Bishop of " Brequin " (Brechin), and others so far as a town which Girard is pleased to call Liscou, but better known as Linlithgow.

The entry took place on the 25th of January ; the ambassadors were lodged at the house " of one Alexander Neppar " ; and there, again, they received the civilities of the same Bishop of " Brequin," of the Lord Privy Seal, of the High Chamberlain, of Sir William Crichton, and many other prelates, knights and esquires. The following day they were received by James in person ; he was staying then in the convent of the Franciscans, according to the wont of the Scotch kings (and other kings too), who lived then as much as they could in convents and friaries, not only in consideration of the holy character of the place, but also because living there cost them nothing. " The Scotch kings,"

writes Pedro de Ayala, " live little in cities and towns.
They pass their time generally in castles and abbeys,
where they find lodgings for all their officers."

James received the ambassadors most honourably ;
he had with him the Bishops of " Abredin " and
" Brequin " (Aberdeen and Brechin), the Earls of
" Glaz " and " Angluz " (Douglas and Angus), and
others whose names were as accurately noted by Regnault Girard.   He listened with great attention to the
message of the chief envoy, who, having had no lack
of time to learn by heart his instructions, explained, we
may believe, with the utmost fidelity, the views of his
master.

But Girard was fated not to find smooth waters
anywhere ; contrary winds arose, and difficulties began.
The questions to be settled were manifold ; first, there
was the marriage itself and the conveying of the young
princess to France, then the question of the French
alliance and the sending of Scotch auxiliaries, the question of the expenses of the home journey of the embassy
and their escort, the question of the English war, and
many other questions.   And there was one more question, not mentioned in the instructions, but which stood
foremost in the mind of James—the question, namely,
of his consenting to part with a beloved and very
youthful daughter, the first-born of a happy marriage,

the favourite child of the queen, that same Jane Beaufort
whom James had loved while a prisoner at Windsor,
and for whom he had composed his delightful " King's
Quhair." The Scotch royal family was a united, loving
family, and from this came the main difficulty the
French ambassadors had to encounter. James was
bound by his word, but it was not forbidden him to
try to postpone at least the fulfilling of it.

First he appointed representatives to discuss matters
with Regnault Girard ; they discussed for six days
together with great zeal, after which they found themselves unable to agree on any point. The affair was
then referred to the king, who said that he could do
nothing without having consulted with the queen. He
thereupon left town and went to " St. Genston "—that
is, St. Johnstown, otherwise Perth—and asked the
ambassadors to meet him there, towards the end of
February.

To Perth the ambassadors repaired accordingly ;
they were presented to the queen, to the future
dauphiness, and to a number of " lady countesses and
baronesses " ; then they resumed their negotiation. A
roll was at last drawn up and signed, which gave them
great satisfaction, and scarcely less to the king, for
there were in it so many clauses and provisoes that it
was impossible not to submit them to the French king

himself, and this meant no little delay. The roll ascribed to France the cost of the " navy " to be purchased and sent to Dumbarton to fetch the princess, the cost also of the " bread, biscuit, beverage, salt and other victuals," to be consumed in the outward journey. The King of Scotland would supply meat, fish, butter, cheese and wood for the homeward journey ; he would bring together two thousand carefully chosen soldiers, the choosing requiring, of course, much time, to accompany the dauphiness and protect her while at sea. Besides, the King of Scotland wanted to know where his daughter would live; she must have a place assigned to her, where a Scotchman would be in command ; and she must be allowed to have Scotch ladies with her. James, however, understood that it was proper for her to have also in her retinue French gentlemen and ladies " to teach her the manners of the country, and to inform her concerning her situation." A galley also, of particular excellence, and carrying crossbowmen and chosen troops, was to be provided, besides the fleet for the two thousand men ; on which galley the princess would take passage. The fleet was bound to reach Dumbarton in May. And so on.

Nothing obviously could be done without the assent of the French king. The envoys resolved that two of them should undertake this additional journey, and go back to La Rochelle. Kennedy and Aymeri Martineau were appointed to do this. Regnault Girard considered that he had better stay ; but his son Joachim went, also Dragance, pursuivant of Scotland, and the four thus departed on Shrove Monday, 1435.

Left alone in Scotland, "which was not without great regret and sorrow" on his part, Regnault Girard established his quarters at Stirling, where the Princess Margaret mostly lived, and having there nothing to do but to wait for the return of his companions, he found the time very long and the winter very dull. James perceived it, and advised the ambassador not to stay at home so much, but to go about and see the country. He provided Girard with people to accompany him, and the French envoy began to visit " several among the good towns of the kingdom, to spend time, and place himself out of the reach of ennui." Girard went thus to Dundee, "where he was greatly feasted by the burgesses," to St. Andrews, where he was handsomely received by the bishop and the prior of the place, and where he had also some intercourse with " those of the university," and to " several other towns and abbeys." He was everywhere welcomed. " To speak truth, in all the places where I went, I was most honourably treated, for the sake of the King of France, and the greatest civilities were shown me as well by churchmen and nobles as by the common people, and they all evinced so much good will in all that concerned the King of France, that I had an impression that nowhere could be found more loyal Frenchmen."

Time thus passed; the appointed date for the coming of the fleet was drawing near, and there was no news of the travellers. Girard then asked King James to take into account the unavoidable impediments which must have stopped them on their way, such as the lack of wind, and to agree that the delay for the coming of the ships might be increased. James had only pleasure in agreeing; and the date of the 20th of September, instead of the end of May, was accepted by him.

In the course of the summer Aymeri Martineau, accompanied by Dragance, the pursuivant of Scotland, came back at last, bringing news of the assent of Charles to several of the conditions proposed, and of his dissent concerning the rest. Somewhat later the other travellers, Kennedy and Joachim Girard, came back also; they had taken passage on the fleet gathered together for the bringing home of the dauphiness, and the said fleet arrived within the delay newly granted by James, and anchored at Dumbarton on the 12th of September " or thereabout."

IV.—THE END OF THE NEGOTIATION.

Aymeri and Kennedy brought letters for Girard and for the King of Scotland. Charles expressed in them his satisfaction at the happy turn taken by the negotiation, congratulated his envoy upon his zeal and cleverness, expressed the joy he had felt on " hearing good news of the good health and prosperity of the King of Scotland, the queen, and their daughter." He agreed to send the navy for two thousand men ; Puver would fulfil his contract, and leave La Rochelle on the 15th of July with his ships ; France would provide bread, biscuit, salt, and wine; Scotland, meat, fish, butter, and cheese. Charles would do his best to secure the wished-for galley meant for the dauphiness. But no such galley could be found in France, and much less in Scotland ; for the art of shipbuilding was not yet a Scottish art, and the hammers were not at work, as they have been since, along the Clyde. Spain was (with Italy) the great shipbuilding country; Charles had sent there special delegates ; but their success was greatly to be doubted, for war was raging " between the Kings of Castile and Arragon. Peace seems to be remote, and no ships, or almost none, are allowed to leave the kingdom of Castile."[1]

[1] For details concerning the Spanish galleys of that date, see Appendix.

Concerning the attendance of the young princess the views of Charles greatly differed from those of his " good brother " James ; for the one wanted Margaret to become as French as possible, and the other wished her to remain as Scotch as could be.   Girard was instructed to do all in his power to lessen the number of people sent to stay with her, to reduce it to nothing if he could, or, at least, to not more than one or two women, and as many men :—" For so long as she will have with her people of her nation, she will not willingly learn French, nor adopt the manners of the French kingdom."   As for a place of safety under the command of a Scottish officer, there was no need for it, for she would stay with the Queen of France, and be treated as if she were a " carnal daughter " of the French House.

Concerning the two thousand men of the escort, the King of France would not deprive his brother of such a valuable force, and they would be sent back to Scotland as soon as the journey was finished.   Charles felt the more at liberty to do so, as affairs had taken a better turn with him ; he had the pleasure to inform James that " his people had recovered the town and abbey of St. Denis, which stands near Paris, also the Pont Sainte-Maxence, upon the Oise river and the town of Rue on the Somme, to the great confusion and diminution of his enemies and adversaries." The Earl of Arundel had been routed, and it was to be hoped that, " by the help of God, the French party would perform great warlike exploits against their foes." The better to show the excellent state of the kingdom where the young princess would have soon to come and live, Charles added, naïvely enough, that he had sent a great many men-at-arms and crossbowmen to Normandy, and beyond the Oise river, to continue the war, " so that he had relieved his provinces of the men-at-arms, and others who wanted to stay and plunder there, by which the state of his people had been greatly improved."

But a more satisfactory piece of information was supplied in a paragraph where Charles stated that " Messeigneurs the Duke de Bourbon, constable of France, the Count de Vendosme, the Chancellor de Harcourt, the Marshal de Lafayette," and others, to the number of a thousand horse or more, had gone " in very great state to the town of Arras," to treat there of peace with the English, in the presence of cardinals sent by the Pope. A sort of European congress, in fact, was meeting at Arras, one of the first on record ; and, whatever should be the outcome of the negotiation, Charles pledged himself to keep his brother of Scotland well informed of everything, and not to sign any arrangement that could in any way slacken the bonds and impair the old-established alliance between France and Scotland. So wrote Charles le Victorieux on the 13th day of July, 1435, when he was staying in his castle of Amboise, on the Loire.

All those papers were communicated to James, then at Stirling. The ambassadors pointed out that the fleet was now ready, and that the time had come to fulfil the " appointments " agreed upon.

But neither James nor the queen could make up their minds to part yet with their daughter. James observed that the fleet had been very slow in coming, that " winter was very near, and that no marriage was allowed during that season between right-minded people." He added that the queen would never be persuaded to consent to it, that the danger from the sea was very great at this time of the year ; " and that we knew full well in what peril we had been ourselves when we came to the land of Scotland." A sly smile accompanied doubtless the delivery of this last observation.

The ambassadors made counter observations, pro-duced other papers ; all proved of no avail. It was at length arranged that Margaret should spend one more winter in her native country, and that towards the March moon her father would trust her " à l'aventure de Dieu."

The fleet, therefore, remained idle at Dumbarton. The king, after some discussion, consented to pay the expenses of this prolonged stay, " no small matter, as it was to last about half a year." Months went on, very slowly in the estimation of the French ambassadors, only too quickly for the royal family of Scotland. The only event which happened in the interval, and has been noted by Girard, was an epidemic among the seamen of the fleet, of whom a great many died.

In February, 1436, towards Candlemas, the envoys betook themselves to the town of "Sainct John Stom" —that is, Perth—to remind the king that " the month of March was now near," and that everything ought to be made ready for the journey. This time James had to consent and to prepare in earnest for the fulfilling of the treaty. A farewell banquet was offered by him to the ambassadors. They sat at the royal table ; the king was there and the queen too, " sitting next him in a chair." It was decided that Girard would go to Dumbarton and see that the fleet were in order, while Kennedy would stay and assist in the choosing of the escort.

The following day another ceremony took place, and a very touching one. The king and queen, the ambassadors being present, ordered the young princess to be brought before them : " They addressed to her several fine words, and memorable ones, reminding her of the honour done to them by the King of France, and of the honour of the prince whom she was to marry. They entreated her to behave well, and God knows the tears which were shed on both sides, while this was going on." The audience having come to an end, the ambassadors took their leave, and the poor father, not knowing how to make Margaret dearer to the French envoy, " for the sake of his brother the King of France, ordered me, Regnault Girard, to kiss the queen, and the queen kindly and gracefully consented, and kissed me : which kiss I repute the greatest honour ever bestowed upon me. We left thereupon."

The day after, fine gifts were sent by James to the house where the ambassadors lodged, and " speaking of this we must not forget that from the day we met him in his town of Edinburgh in the realm of Scotland, which was the 25th of January, 1435, we were defrayed by him of all our ordinary expenses, wheresoever we went."

Girard and his son, as well as Aymeri Martineau, left Perth on the 15th of February, 1436, and went to the ships to consult with the seamen. They saw that all would be got ready for the first tides of the March moon, and in order the better to attend to the business, honest Regnault Girard, bad sailor as he was, went on board at once and there remained : "and I kept the sea for fifteen days before the king came, and I felt great discomforts."

While he was thus tossing on the water a ship came from France, with goods to enable him to offer in his turn presents to the Scotch king. Whatever may have been the gifts of James, the ambassadorial ones were of primæval simplicity. They consisted first of a gentle mule––"ung mullet bien gent"––whom "I had ordered by the advice of Monseigneur de Vendosme, who had spoken to me about it when I took the sea, for he had seen the mule himself at La Rochelle. This mule I caused to be offered to the King of Scotland ; and he received it with great joy, and it was considered a very strange animal, for there are none in that country. As for the queen, I caused her to be presented with three casks full of fruit, such as pears, apples, chestnuts, and others, and with six casks of wine ; and she was very happy to have them, for there is very little fruit in Scotland."

V.—THE HOMEWARD JOURNEY.

At last, at the beginning of March, the army as well as the fleet being ready, the king came with the dauphiness to Dumbarton, and with the noblemen who were

4

to accompany her, such as the Bishop of Brechin, the Count " Derquenay "—that is, the Earl of Orkney— and other gentlemen whose names are equally trans- formed by the pen of Girard.   One last thing James would do before trusting Margaret " à l'aventure de Dieu," and in this his fatherly anxieties appeared again. " One day the king came to see the ships, and he wanted to have a trial of them, and he ordered them to sail, so that he might ascertain which of them was fastest and best appointed to carry our said lady.   And he found me there, on the ships, and he treated me wonderfully well and honourably."   A sort of race was thus run in the presence of James, and it turned out that the swiftest ship was the one belonging to Peter Chepye (Percipey as he is called by Bower, whose narrative closely agrees on many points with Girard's). " It was a new one and an excellent sailer, and had been built in the kingdom of Spain ; it was agreed that our whaler would constantly keep by the said ship, to help and protect our lady in case of need.   Of which whaler my son Joachim Girard had command."

James having thus arranged matters and left the ships, " the masters of the same were not at all pleased with the arrangements taken by him, and they began to discuss the question noisily among themselves.   They came to me, and said that in all the fleet there was but one Spanish ship, and that all the rest hailed from France and Brittany ; that it would put to shame all the masters of those ships to suffer that our lady the dauphiness took passage on the ship of Peter Chepye, that they would not allow it for any consideration, that they would fight Chepye as soon as they were in the open sea, whatever be the decision of the King of Scotland, and that the said Chepye would not have the honour of carrying their mistress, Madame la Dauphine."

An additional danger of an unexpected sort was thus threatening the princess, and who knows what might have happened if the impending fight had taken place ? Regnault Girard displayed again in this occurrence the resources of his diplomatic mind ; he tried his best to pacify the seamen, he spoke soothing words, and as these would not suffice—" for sailors are very difficult to manage, and they magnify things to a wonder "—he promised them that as soon as they should be out of view of the Scottish coast he would put the princess into the whaler, " and thus the French fleet would have the honour of carrying her, and by this means I pacified them."

On the 27th of March the king came for the last time. He had his daughter with him. He saw her on board the ship of Peter Chepye, ordered Girard and

Aymeri Martineau to take passage with her ; the Earl of Orkney, the Bishop of Brechin, and other noblemen, and a number of chosen archers came into the same boat. Hugh Kennedy was in command of one of the warships called *Saint-Gille*. The officers, soldiers, and archers of the escort went on board their respective ships. Everything being thus arranged, and no cause or pretext remaining for a more prolonged stay, the poor father had to take his leave ; " the king did not stay long, but went away weeping many tears, for the sorrow of his leaving our lady the dauphiness his daughter."

The fleet weighed anchor ; the number of warships was eleven, containing about one thousand or twelve hundred men, all of them chosen Scottish soldiers, without speaking of the sailors manning the fleet, who were French. The weather was favourable for one day and night, then contrary winds arose, and, instructed by experience, and not at all desirous to risk the worst, the ambassadors ordered the fleet to go back, and they stopped for a little while in a harbour of Scotland. Then the wind turned, and they put to sea again, and they had fine weather during all the rest of the passage, " thanks be to God, and we came in view of La Palice, not far from La Rochelle, on the 17th of April ; and on the following day we reached Chef-

THE TOWER WITH THE CHAIN AT THE ENTRANCE OF LA ROCHELLE HARBOUR.

de-Baye, at a distance of about one league from the said town."

The intention had been to have the city of La Rochelle prepared and adorned against the coming of the princess. Margaret would remain in her ship— which ship it was, whether Peter Chepye's or the whaler, we do not know—till the town was ready. But a tempest interfered with the ceremonial ; it was so sudden and terrific that the boat carrying Margaret had to be conveyed without any delay to the inner harbour of the town ; the other ships did for the best, and drew near the great tower with the chain (still in existence—we give a view of it) ; but in so doing, one of the ships, built in Brittany, " was greatly wounded." On that day " our lady was not shown to the people, because it was late and the town was not decorated." The day after, at early dawn, before she could be seen by any one, she was taken to a neighbouring abbey, and there waited till the Rochelle people had had time so to adorn their town that a princess might decently make an entry into it.

She received in the meanwhile the visit of several great men sent by the king to congratulate her upon her coming ; among them was the chancellor of the kingdom, this same Regnault de Chartres, archbishop-duke of Reims, who had gone nine years before to Scotland to ask for the hand of the same Margaret.

On the 10th of May, 1436, all was at last ready, and Margaret, retracing her steps, went back to La Rochelle, accompanied by a splendid retinue of Scottish men-at-arms, French noblemen of the region, special envoys of the king, &c. She was welcomed by the mayor and the guilds ; a little further on by the ladies and burgesses, and then " she received a fine present of silver plate, which she greatly liked, as it was the first she received in this kingdom."

Then she went to Niort, where she was complimented by the Lady Perrette de la Rivière, dame de la Roche Guyon, first lady of honour to the queen, and by Blanche de Gamaches, dame de Chastillon, another lady of honour ; she passed other towns where she was received in great state and presented with fine gifts. At Poictiers brilliant festivities had been prepared for her ; the mayor and notables came out of the town to the distance of more than one league; after this she was met by gentlemen belonging to the Court of Parliament, then by the doctors and students of the University, and by representatives of various dignified bodies. " While she was entering the town a child, disguised as an angel, was let down from the portal of the city, and placed a chapel (crown) on her head, a thing which was most genteelly and craftily performed." At the main crossings, according to the custom of the time, Margaret, whose thoughts were, perhaps, far away, lingering over the beloved remote places where her childhood was spent, had to admire a variety of allegorical personages, richly apparelled, and to listen to numerous complimentary addresses.

While this was going on Girard went to Bourges, where the king was, to render account of all that had taken place, and receive instructions for the marriage. He was graciously treated by the king, who congratulated him upon the success of his embassy, and appointed that the marriage should take place at Tours, on the day after the feast of St. John the Baptist.

All concerned met then at Tours. The king arrived on the morning of the nuptials, and, as the manners of the time allowed, went, in order to ascertain how his daughter-in-law looked, "into her room while she was being dressed. He was greatly pleased with her person, and felt great joy at the sight." So says Regnault Girard, and well he might, as Margaret was, according to Mathieu d'Escouchy, "beautiful and well shaped, and adorned with all the qualities befitting a noble and high lady."

Soon after the princess, wearing the crown, was

taken to the door of the church, and there she met and saw for the first time the prince who was to be her husband, according to the arrangements signed when she was three years old. Young Louis wore the royal garb, and was followed by the princes of the blood. The marriage was at once blessed and consecrated by the Archbishop of Reims. "Great was the feast," writes Regnault Girard, who abstains from giving any details. Not so great, however, for the town accounts have survived centuries and revolutions, and we still know exactly what the good men of Tours spent to welcome the Lady Dauphiness. They had had little time to get ready, and all they could do is commemorated in the following entries :—

Firstly, to Robin Lebarbier, sent to Chinon and to Loudun, to try and find dresses for a play to be played on the joyful coming of my Lady the Dauphiness, for his expenses and the hiring of his horse   ...   .   35 sols.

To Richard Gaugain, for four old bed sheets, used to make three dresses for those who shall dance the morris before my lady ...   15 sols.

To Jean Avisart, tailor, who cut, sewed, and made the said dresses   ...   .   15 sols.

To Denis, the painter-glazier, for having

hastily and richly painted those dresses, and
four beards for the same dancers   ...   ...   40 sols.

To Gervaise Lechanteur, for twenty-seven
dozens of bells, distributed among the said
dancers and the taborer   ...   .   30 sols.

To the same, for the hiring of part of
those bells, which were afterwards returned...   5 sols.

To André Hacqueteau, saddler, who sewed
on leather the said bells, for them to be
placed on the hands and legs of the dancers   5s. 6d.

To two women who had gathered flowers
to make head-wreaths for the said men   ...   2s. 6d.

To Pierre Rossignol (nightingale) and his
companions, minstrels, who sounded their
horns in the hat market on the coming of my
lady ...   .   10 sols.

To four fellows who built a scaffold on the
drawbridge of the bulwark of Our-Lady-the
Rich, where the organs were. . . . To four
fellows who brought there and back the said
organs   ...   .   3s. 4d.

To master Robert-the-Devil, one of the
dancers, for his trouble, and for having
ordained the said dance ; for having attended
to the making and painting of the dresses, and
for a pair of hose which he asserted to have
burst while dancing ...   .   30 sols.

We shall stop here our quotations, not without some suspicion that master Robert-the-Devil who put forth such assertions, which the town accountant only half endorses, well deserved, maybe, his nickname. As for the others, the items concerning them give a clear idea of what took place, and we see how the inhabitants did their best, having so little time, to get up a play, tried to find ready-made dresses, failed, and had to be content with a morris dance, the dancers being "richly and hastily" apparelled in dresses cut out of old bed sheets, and tinkling all over with their twenty-seven dozens of little bells sewed on their arms and legs. This sound was accompanied by the music of the church organ, brought out into the open air for the occasion. They carry flowers on their heads, they dance and jump, they make merry, and Robert-the-Devil distinguishes himself and bursts his hose, "as he asserts."

The men from Scotland were handsomely treated; they received "fine gifts" which remain nondescript in the "Relation" of Girard, now drawing to its close. A few of her compatriots were allowed to stay with Margaret. Regnault Girard was appropriately appointed her first master of the hostel, and Joachim the esquire of her stables.

"And thus came to an end the embassy sent to

fetch from the kingdom of Scotland our most redoubted and mighty lady, Margaret, eldest daughter of the king of the kingdom of Scotland, Dauphiness of Viennois— Thus signed : Regnault—Hue Crenedi—Aymeri Martineau.''

VI.—THE END.

Festive days passed. The daughter of the Stuarts was not long in discovering the sort of man she had been married to. Beautiful and kind, bred at the fireside of a loving father and mother, endowed herself with a loving nature, fond of art and poetry, she found herself tied for life to a man without a heart, who never cared for father, mother, or wife, and whose only interest in life was political ambition. The historian Commines has thus summed up his opinion concerning the tastes and inclinations of his hero : " He was very fond of falcons, but not quite so much as he was of dogs. As for ladies, he never cared for them."

Poor Margaret, deserted by her husband, tried to find some alleviation to her sorrows, and used the means which had been the resource of her father many years before, when he was a captive in England. She read books and wrote poetry. But she could not forget her grief ; gnawing thoughts preyed upon her ; vile calumnies brought her to the verge of despair.   She could no longer rest nor sleep, but sat on her bed, musing, regretting the dear, far-off mother-country.   " Were it not for my pledged word," she said once, " I would fain regret having ever left Scotland."

The king and queen loved her dearly, and did all they could to soothe her.   They lived with her as much as possible ; they tried to amuse her ; they said that she should not " mérencolier " herself so.   The king once inquired why she looked so pale ; a friend of Louis hastened to answer that the cause was that she overworked herself.   " She would," he said, " write roundels, and busy herself so much with such work, that she would write as many as twelve in a day ; a thing which is most unwholesome for her."

" What ! " said the king, " does such writing give headaches ? "

" Yes," answered Jean Bureau, who happened to be there, " to those who overdo it, though such things are only trifles."

Years went on, Louis forsook her more and more, she looked paler and paler ; she was fading away. She died at Châlons on the 16th of August, 1445, a heartbroken, childless wife, being then only twenty.[1]

---

[1] The author of the " Liber Pluscardensis " (ed. Skene, Edinburgh, 1877–80, vol. i. p. 382 ; ii. p. 288), who was with her in

And this was the real end of " the embassy sent to
fetch from the kingdom of Scotland our most redoubted
and mighty lady, Margaret, daughter of the king of
the kingdom of Scotland, Dauphiness of Viennois."

France, thus concludes his notice of her : " Here follows her
epitaph which was placed upon her tomb after her death, in the
French tongue ; only it is here translated into the Scottish
tongue, by command of that Lady's brother, King James II., of
famous memory :

> " He michti makar of the major munde,
>   Quhilk reuly rollis thir hevinly regionis rownd
>   About this erd, be mocioune circuler,
>   Ger all the cloudis of the hevin habound,
>   And souk vp all thir watteris hal and sounde,
>   Baith of salt sey, of burne, well and revere ;
>   Syn to discende in tygglande teris tere,
>   To weip with me this wofull waymentyng,
>   This petwys playnt of a princes but peire,
>   Quhilk dulfull Deed has tane till his duelling." [etc.]

Another daughter of James, Isabel, spent her life in France,
having married the Duke of Brittany. Her Book of Hours was
recently purchased by the National Library, Paris (Nouvelles
acquisitions, 588). Her portrait is to be seen at fol. 33.

III.

PAUL SCARRON.

I.—THE CRIPPLE.

GREAT things were done in the days of the Grand Roi. Mighty efforts were made to rule an unruly kingdom, the France of the League and the Fronde. Battles were won (some it is true were lost) ; tragedies were written, porticoes were built ; Nature herself had to submit to the sway of the monarch, and trees rose " en charmilles," at Versailles and elsewhere.

Let us not believe, however, that only porticoes were built in France at that time, that only tragedies were written, obeying the stern rules of the three unities, and that no novels were published but the huge compositions of Madeleine de Scudéry, telling the wonderful exploits of the Grand Cyrus. Not all trees, in fact, were cut according to pattern ; all plays did not obey the three rules ; men were found who did not wear a wig : so difficult it is to establish order in a country. Novels even were written, containing accurate pictures of plain everyday life. Three at least can be named. One is by Madame de La Fayette, who gave in her " Princesse de Clèves," 1678, an inimitable picture of court society ; another is the work of Furetière, whose " Roman Bourgeois" is an excellent description of middle-class life in 1666 ; the third and earliest in date, the most curious of the three, is the " Roman Comique," 1651, of Scarron, who chose the difficult task of depicting provincial France.

Paul Scarron was the son of a " conseiller au Parlement," and was born in Paris in 1610. Paul Scarron, the father, was a man of importance and belonged to a good family with aristocratic alliances. When contemporaries (Mathieu Molé, for one) allude to the presence or sayings of councillors, they usually name him among those to be noticed. He was even exiled by order of Louis XIII.,[1] so much attention was paid to his doings. He was a whimsical man, nicknamed " the Apostle " by

---

[1] "Le Lundi 30 Janvrier [1640] j'ai présenté à la cour des lettres de jussion du roi sur le refus de vérification par le Parlement de l'édit de création de seize Maîtres des requêtes. . . . L'édit a encore été refusé. . . . M. Scarron [eut commandment] de s'en aller en sa maison vers Blois." " Mémoires de Mathieu Molé" (Société de l'Histoire de France), ii. p. 475. Cf. Bassompierre's " Mémoires" (p. by the same Society), iv. p. 328

Prince de Condé on account of his constant reading of the Epistles of St. Paul his patron. He was a passionate admirer of Ronsard and could never forgive his son who preferred Malherbe. The poet's mother died when he was still young, and, his father having re-married, family life, instead of being thus renewed, turned out to be definitively broken for the future poet. When he reached the age of man he began on his own account, and for the sake of his sisters, a long war with his stepmother, a rapacious and tyrannical woman. The war, initiated at home in his father's time, was continued long after, and had for its seat sometimes the courts of law and sometimes the booksellers' shops in the "Galeries du Palais." No good came out of it for any one, both parties finding themselves when it was finished sore and bruised and the poorer for it.

Scarron was first destined to the Church and was, from 1633, for many years, known as l'abbé Scarron. At this time he resided at Le Mans, in the house of the bishop, Monseigneur Charles de Beaumanoir, leading, however, no exemplary life, mixing with the gayest company, associating with players—in fact, preparing himself much more to write of l'Étoile and Destin than to become a Church dignitary. He was then gaiety itself, lithe and active. He wrote agreeable verses, was a good dancer, played on the lute, and was an amateur painter of skill. At all the neighbouring châteaux, especially among the Lavardin and Tessé families, he was a welcome guest.

In 1635 Monseigneur de Beaumanoir had to go to Rome and did not fail to take there with him the lively abbé, who was sure to prove a very acceptable travelling companion. In Rome Scarron improved his acquaintance with painting and painters. Players and painters were ever among his best friends. He met there his famous compatriots, Nicolas Poussin and Pierre Mignard, and he began with them an intercourse which lasted through life. It was one of the peculiarities of his mind : with all his love of the grotesque and the burlesque, he had in his heart a veneration for higher things ; he felt and understood them. His admiration for the austere genius of Poussin was boundless. In the same way as the Grand Roi, though being the Grand Roi, would enjoy " Pourceaugnac," the first representation of which was reserved for his applause, so Scarron, though being Scarron, had a passion for the author of " Les Bergers d'Arcadie," now in the Louvre, as well as for the classical poetry of Malherbe. Those contradictory tastes were frequent at that time ; people were not so stiff and one-sided as they are sometimes supposed to have been ; real birds are known to have perched on the yew-trees at Versailles.

5

In the case of Poussin, however, Scarron's passion got only a poor return. Nothing is more curious and characteristic of the man than the circumlocutions and precautions to which kindly, modest Poussin resorted in order to avoid expressing too sharply the feelings that he entertained towards the author of the "Virgile Travesti." He, for one, had no contradictory tastes, and could not be induced to deride what he at the same time adored. This Scarron could do ; for all the travesty he put on the shoulders of Virgil, he none the less at bottom adored him, as everybody did in his day. His work was a joke, and he wanted his readers to take it as nothing more than a *gaminerie*. He knew full well, and was ready to agree, that if it was to be considered in any other light, it could not but appear sacrilegious. "Mon très Révérend Père," he wrote once to a reverend father in the Church, "I have heard from you that Father Vavasseur has written against burlesque style. . . . As I am in a way the cause of the country having been flooded by works in that style, Father Vavasseur might as well have called me to account on that score. Those who believe I should have been angry do not understand me." [1]   Poussin

---

[1] "Vous m'avez appris que le Père Vavasseur avait écrit contre le style burlesque. Il a bien fait. . . . Puisque je suis cause en quelque façon du grand débordement qui s'en est fait, le Père

was among those who "did not understand" Scarron ;
in the eyes of the painter the burlesque poet was
nothing else than a "new Erostrates." Each mis-
took the other's temper. Scarron thought he would
be of service to Poussin in making him laugh, and
he never forgot to send him any new book of his
which he considered a laughable one. Poussin, in his
turn, being asked by Scarron for a picture would paint
a bacchanal, but Scarron preferred to obtain from the
high-minded artist something in his highest style and
he insisted upon Poussin painting for him a "Ravissement de Saint Paul." Poor Poussin was wont then to
open his heart to his friend, M. de Chantelou, to whom
he would write in this strain : "I have received from
the master of the French post a ridiculous book containing the facetiæ of M. Scarron. . . . I perused
the book once and will not open it again ; you will
pardon me if I do not express to you in full the deep
disgust I feel for such works." [1]

Vavasseur n'aurait peut-être pas mal fait de s'en prendre à moi.
Ceux qui vous ont dit que j'en étais en colère contre lui ne me
connaissent pas." "Les Dernières Œuvres de M. Scarron," Paris,
1740 (first edition, 1663), 2 vols. 12mo, i. p. 181.

[1] "J'ai reçu du maître de la poste de France un livre ridicule
des facéties de M. Scarron. . . . J'ai parcouru ce livre une seule
fois et c'est pour toujours : vous trouverez bon que je ne vous
exprime pas tout le dégoût que j'ai pour de pareils ouvrages."
Rome, February 4, 1647. "Collection des Lettres de Nicolas
Poussin," Paris, 1824, 8vo, p. 256.

The next year Scarron sends to Poussin his " Typhon "
and " threatens " him with his " Virgile Travesti "; upon
which the painter writes again scrrowfully to his friend :
" I had already written to M. Scarron, in answer to the
letter which I got from him with his ' Typhon ' in
burlesque style ; but the one I have just received with
yours is for me a new cause of trouble.   I wish he
would desist and end by liking my paintings as little as
I like his burlesque.   I am sorry he took the trouble
to send me his work ; but the worst of all is that he
threatens me with a travestied Virgil of his own, and
with an epistle directed to me, which he means to print
in the next book he publishes.   He aims, he says, at
making me laugh as heartily as he does himself, cripple
as he is ; but on the contrary I am near weeping when
I think a new Erostrates has been born in our country.
I tell you this in confidence ; do not let him know.
I shall write to him in a different strain, and try
to please him, at least in words."   January 12, 1648.[1]

The next year we find Poussin at work on a " sujet
bachique pour M. Scarron."   But Scarron never received
it, as it seems ; he got another instead, painted to his
order : " I shall be able to send at the same time to
M. l'abbé Scarron the picture I painted for him of the
' Ravissement ' of St. Paul.   You will see it, and will

[1] P. 282.

be so good as to tell me your sentiment about it."
Everybody is now able to see it and to express his
" sentiment about it," for the picture is in the Louvre
and was long in no less a place than the " Salon Carré "
itself.[1] It is the more interesting as it shows the great
influence Domenichino had on Poussin : the admiration of the Frenchman for the Italian is well known ;
in this particular case Poussin seems to have taken his
inspiration direct from his master, whose picture representing the same subject of St. Paul carried to heaven
by angels is also in the Louvre.

Scarron had come back to France in 1636, and had
been put in possession of a canonry at Le Mans, where
he seems to have resumed his former gay life. But
the time had arrived when it was to be stopped. Not
long after his return began that strange disease which
baffled all attempts to cure or even explain it. It was a
progressive malady which got possession of him little
by little, attacking his feet, then his legs, then his arms
and afterwards his fingers ; he became a paralytic and a
cripple, as helpless as he had been agile before ; he lost
sleep and suffered strange flashes of pain, the usual ac-
companiment of diseases of the spine. His sufferings

---

[1] See a reproduction of it in " The Comical Romance and other
Tales by Paul Scarron," London, Lawrence and Bullen, 1892,
vol i. p. viii.

increased as he grew older ; towards the end he could scarcely write. "The extreme tip of my fingers," he said, "is the place of abode of a legion of black devils."

> "De mes cinq doigts l'extrême région
> De démons noirs loge une légion." [1]

"Pour moi," he wrote on another occasion to the Comte de Vivonne, "I am constantly getting worse, and I feel I am gliding towards my end at a quicker pace than I should like ; I have a thousand pains, or rather a thousand legions of devils in my arms and legs." [2] For a long time he could not patiently submit to what was then an almost unexampled fate ; sometimes he tried remedies, and sometimes he thought of suicide : "When I think," he wrote to Marigny, "that my mind is not weak, that I have neither ambition nor avarice, and that, if the powers above had left me the use of legs which used to dance pretty well and of hands which knew how to paint and play the lute, the use, in a word, of a very agile body, I might have led a happy though rather obscure life, I assure you, my dear friend, that were it allowed me to get rid of my own existence I should have poisoned myself long ago." [3]

He tried the waters, experimented with strange pills

[1] "Dernières Œuvres," p. 240. Epistre à M. Pellisson.
[2] June 12, 1660 (shortly before his death), "Dernières Œuvres," i. p. 55.   [3] *Ibid.*, p. 61.

and queer baths; but with no effect. In 1641 and 1642 he underwent a cure at Bourbon, and there found himself the king of the sick :—" Many people have I seen, ugly and pretty, good and wicked, wealthy and poor, tall and short, all of them more or less disabled, but I can safely say, and without self-conceit, that there I was in my own kingdom ; and that everybody paid homage to me as being sick above them all. All their diseases put together are trifling when compared to mine. My body is no longer a human body ; my skin is a sort of dry vellum, a sieve through which my bones are cutting holes."

> " Certes, j'ai vu maintes personnes,
> Laides, belles, mauvaises, bonnes,
> Pauvres, riches, petits et grands
> Et tous assez mal se portans :
> Mais sans vanité je puis dire
> Que là j'étais dans mon empire,
> Et que tous m'y portaient honneur
> Comme a leur malade majeur.
> Aussi tous leurs maux joints ensemble
> Près des miens sont peu ce me semble.
> Mon corps n'est plus un corps humain ;
> Sa peau n'est qu'un sec parchemin
> Dont mes os veulent faire un crible." [1]

This kingship he retained all his life, and so sure was he after a while that he would not be dispossessed

[1] " Seconde Légende de Bourbon." " Œuvres," 1786, 7 vol. 8vo, vii. p. 13.

of it that he received only with laughter the news of the coming of a certain Spanish paralytic to make "assaut de réputation" against him.[1]

The mystery of this strange disease has been recently explained. The eminent surgeon, Professor Lannelongue, whom I consulted about Scarron, kindly wrote to me as follows :—"Not another day must I put off the poor fellow who has been unable for two hundred years to find some proper information concerning his disease. My diagnosis will be the more useful as it will wash his memory from a charge brought against him by his contemporaries.[2] The least informed are often the worst accusers. Scarron seems to me to have suffered from a tuberculous affection of the vertebræ, what we now call Pott's disease. At the time of life when he was seized with it—that is, when he had reached maturity—this disease assumes usually an insidious character ; it is slowly progressive, and leads to paralysis, and to a contraction of the muscles, distorting the limbs of the sufferer in the way you have described to me. Shootings of pain are another important symptom of the malady. Scarron must have died marasmatic, though keeping his intelligence unimpaired" (Valmont, September 30, 1891).

[1] Letter to Marigny, "Dernières Œuvres," *ut supra*, p. 62.
[2] See Tallemant's "Historiette" concerning "le petit Scarron."

Scarron was now settled in Paris, in the Quartier du Marais, not far from the Place Royale where Ninon de Lenclos lived, and Madame de Sévigné had been born, and many people with a name in the annals of literature and fashion had established themselves. It has greatly altered since. Compared with the Luxembourg or the Parc Monceau, with their wealth of flowers and the rich foliage of their trees, the square in the Place Royale, now called Place des Vosges, with its meagre plants and thin trees, with its noisy children and dusty benches, with its dogs and cats, seems to-day a bit of " province " transplanted into the middle of the capital.

After a while Scarron had to leave what was then a very elegant quarter and go beyond the water to the Faubourg St. Germain, there to try a new remedy. It was one of those extraordinary panaceas meant to heal any disease, and such as the fertile mind of the Purgons and Diafoirus of the time, not yet broken by their arch-enemy Molière, was wont to invent. Of which panacea and journey to the " rive gauche " thus writes the poor poet : " Good-bye, fine Quartier du Marais. With many regrets I have to leave you for a while at the call of a pressing necessity. I am going to the Faubourg St. Germain, to dip that dry vellum my skin into a bath said to be the best thing to cure

the pains which make me howl. . . . I must go, not
on my legs, for my feet are of no use to me, and bathe
myself in a gutter, for gutter may I well call the bath
prepared for me, as it is a bath of guts." [1]

And then he says good-bye to all his friends one by
one: Adieu, "Lady who art everybody's talk, charming Ninon, beautiful Ninon.   Adieu, ditto, beautiful de
Lorme " :

> "Fille dont parle tout le monde,
> Charmant esprit, belle Ninon . . .
> Item adieu belle de Lorme ; "

Adieu to this one and adieu to that other.[2]   While
he is carried on his chair over the bridge he looks from
the windows : " From the chair in which I am carried,

---

[1] " Adieu, beau quartier du Marets !
　　C'est avecque mille regrets
　　Qu'une très pressante besoigne
　　Pour quelque temps de vous m'éloigne.
　　Je vais au faubourg St. Germain
　　Tremper mon très sec parchemin
　　Dans un bain qu'on tient salutaire
　　A la douleur qui me fait braire. . . .
　　Je veux aller, non de mon pas,
　　Car des pieds j'ai perdu l'usage,
　　Me baigner dans un tripotage :
　　Car tripotage appeler puis
　　Le bain auquel destiné suis
　　Puis qu'il est composé de tripes."

[2] " Adieux aux Marais," " Œuvres," vii. p. 29.

how many people I see walking ! What would I not give to be able to walk too ! "

> " Que de la chaise qui me porte
> J'aperçois de gens cheminer !
> Hélas ! que me faut-il donner
> Pour pouvoir marcher de la sorte ? " [1]

But, alas ! he was not destined to walk any more ; the " bain de tripes " proved of no avail ; he had to dream of other inventions and began studying Raymond Lulle. Send me, he writes to a friend, " all you will be able to find by Raymond Lulle ; I will return you the money when you come to Paris. . . . I have been worse than ever during the last fortnight and I trust in nothing but in potable gold." [2]

Chemists and alchemists equally failed, and we find one day poor Scarron confessing that the only thing which did him any real good was—to swear ! In this he had such faith (and experience) that he went the length of recommending it to his friends in trouble as a most efficacious and at all events accessible remedy. " I swear, without pride, as well as any one in France, and I believe that if his Highness would condescend to

---

[1] "Le Chemin du Marais au faubourg St. Germain," " Œuvres," vii. p. 233.

[2] "Dernières Œuvres," i. p. 50. Concerning this friend, see below, p. 96.

swear sometimes like a man it would do him no harm. . . . As for me, I am sometimes in such a passion that if all the devils were willing to come and fetch me, I think I would go half way to meet them."[1]

Scarron had now taken apartments in the "Hôtel de Troyes," Rue d'Enfer, not far from the Luxembourg.[2] He had furnished his rooms with taste and in a costly fashion. Some parts of his person had not been disabled by the malady, and he tried to avail himself of those and to live an acceptable, though fragmentary, sort of a life. His stomach remained good, and his friends supplied him with wine from the country, cheeses, tarts, and pasties. What, however, he did enjoy most and above everything was the unimpeded agility of his mind. His ideas remained clear, his wit kept all its sharpness, his temper all its gaiety. Broken as he was in his body, sleepless and a constant sufferer, he was always ready for a joke, the equal of any one in conversation, so gay, so pleasant, so good-humoured, that all Paris flocked to his rooms to see the wonder,

[1] "Dernières Œuvres," i. p. 63.

[2] Concerning the various places of abode of Scarron, see A. de Boislisle's "Paul Scarron et Françoise d'Aubigné," a reprint from the "Revue des Questions Historiques," Paris, 1894, pp. 31 *seq.* Concerning especially the Hôtel de Troyes, see pp. 34 and 179.

and to amuse the poor fellow and be amused by him. There is scarcely any other example of so much acute pain so lightly borne, with such an ease indeed that not only did he make his company bearable—which is the most disabled people usually can do—but sought for and enjoyed. Men and women of fashion, maréchaux de France and précieuses, men of letters and men of the sword, players and painters, were seen from day to day in his apartment. They came, and what they saw Scarron himself has described. It was then the fashion to write portraits ; Madame de La Fayette drew some, Mademoiselle de Scudéry many ; there are constant allusions to them in Madame de Sévigné's letters. Here is the portrait of Scarron drawn by himself in the year 1648 :

" Reader, who have never seen me, and possibly do not want to, for there can be no great pleasure in seeing a creature made as I am, be sure that I would not much like you to see me, had I not heard that certain facetious wits are making jokes at my expense, and give unfaithful descriptions of how I am built. Some pretend that I am a cripple sitting in a wooden bowl, others that I have no thighs, and that people put me into a sheath, and on a table, where I chatter like a magpie ; and others assert that my hat hangs to a rope by which I raise or lower it to welcome visitors. I think I am bound in conscience to prevent them lying any longer : and with this object I had the plate made which you see in front of my book.[1]   You will grumble, doubtless ; I grumble too when I am a reader ; you will grumble, I say, and find fault, because I show myself only from behind.   It is not, I protest, because I want to turn my back upon the company, but merely because the roundness of my back is better fitted to receive an inscription than the hollow of my stomach ; the same being, besides, partly concealed by my leaning head. . . . Without pretending that I should by this means have bestowed any great gift upon the public (for, by our ladies the Nine Sisters, I never hoped that my head might be used as a model for a medal), I should have willingly ordered my portrait to be painted, but no painter could be expected to attempt such a task.   Failing a picture I shall tell you how I am made.

"I am now over thirty, as you see on the back of my chair.[2]   If I reach forty, I shall add many sufferings

---

[1] See a reproduction of it in "The Comical Romance, and other Tales by Paul Scarron."   London, Lawrence and Bullen, 1892, vol. ii.

[2] He was much older, as he was writing in 1648, having been born in 1610.   Some biographers' supposition that Della Bella's engraving used as a frontispiece to Scarron's volume was made in 1641 cannot be admitted, for the plate was meant to adorn a poem on the death of Voiture, which took place in 1648.   Besides what

to those I have borne for the last eight or nine years. Though not tall, I had formerly a rather good figure ; disease has made it now shorter by a foot. My head is a little large for my height . . . my sight is pretty good though my eyes be big ones ; they are blue . . . my teeth, square pearls in former years, have now a wooden colour, and will soon be slate-coloured . . . my legs and thighs made at first an obtuse angle, then a right angle ; now they make an acute one ; my body and thighs make another, and as my head leans over my stomach I am very like a Z. My arms have been shortened as well as my legs ; and my fingers as well as my arms ; in a word I present an abstract of all human miseries."

Of his temper he writes with the same minute exactitude : "I was ever a little choleric, a little *gourmand*, and a little lazy. I often call my servant an ass, and soon after address him as *monsieur*. I hate nobody ; may I be similarly treated ! I am glad when I have money, and would be more glad if I had health. I am rather pleased when I have company ; I am not

Scarron says here of the date when his disease began squares with the indication in " 'Typhon," when he refers to it as having begun in 1638. If he had been only thirty-one when he wrote the lines above and referred to the plate, the date of his illness would be 1632 or 1633, which we know to be wrong, as he was able after that time to travel in Italy.

displeased when I am alone ; I bear my sufferings rather patiently." [1]

The plate he ordered as a frontispiece to a volume of his works in 1648 is a very curious one, and was drawn according to his own directions. Faithful to his tastes in artistic matters, he applied to a classical engraver to have it made, and it looks strange and queer among the grand landscapes, conventional trees and carefully drawn ruins which abound in the works of Della Bella.

People came in and talked. Scarron was one of the great talkers of his day ; I am, he said himself, " un des grands parleurs que je connaisse." [2] We need not inquire whether the sort of talk was of the freest ; the late abbé who still remembered his gay life of former days was not the man to stop the mouth of any visitor. All sorts of freedom and libertinage were allowed in the yellow-damask rooms ; certain subjects with which he could now busy himself only in thought constantly recurred, without which he asserted, " all conversation is sure to die before very long." [3] Political questions, religious questions, literary questions,

---

[1] " La Relation véritable de tout ce qui s'est passé dans l'autre Monde au Combat des Parques et des Poètes sur la mort de Voiture." Paris, 1648, 4to.

[2] " Dernières Œuvres," i. p. 37.

[3] To Vivonne, " Dernières Œuvres," i. p. 198

manners and fashions were discussed with an equally free mind. Retz was among the more devoted frequenters of Scarron's rooms and both spoke all that came into their head, " when he leaned beside me on my little yellow bed and discussed other topics than the Fronde . . . I can pride myself upon having obliged him to set aside the gravity and haughtiness usually associated with the red hat." [1] They did not, however, forbear to speak also of the Fronde, and bitter sarcasms, epigrams, pungent jokes, at the expense of Mazarin, sprang by thousands during those stormy times from the " Hôtel de Troyes," and supplied the Frondeurs with what proved not the least effectual of their ammunitions. A number of anonymous pamphlets were for this cause attributed to Scarron ; one of them, the most scurrilous of all, "La Mazarinade" (March 11, 1651), was the cause of a persistent ill-will of the all-powerful Cardinal towards the poet. Scarron protested and denied the pamphlet, but in vain.[2] If he was not the author of it 'he was the

---

[1] To Fouquet, " Dernières Œuvres," i. p. 104.

[2] " Cent Quatre Vers contre ceux qui font passer leurs Libelles difamatoires sous le nom d'autrui, par M. Scarron." Paris, Quinet, 1651. See also his " Dernières Œuvres," i. p. 202 : " Pendant les troubles de la Régence, ma malheureuse réputation a été cause que tout ce qu'on a imprimé à Paris de bon et de méchant a été publié sous mon nom, et cet abus dure encore. . . ."

inspirer of many such, as was only too apparent from the number of *mazarinades* where " Scarron's muse " was called to the rescue.[1]

On important occasions he had himself carried to other people's houses and paid a visit in person. He did it once for the Queen Mother, another time for Christina, the Queen of Sweden, several times for Ninon de Lenclos. From his visit to Anne of Austria he brought back the title of the Queen's own "malade" and a pension,[2] and he was wont in after time to sign himself " le malade de la Reine." He went to the Louvre again "pour contenter la curiosité" of Christina, to whom he addressed several eulogistic letters and dedicated one of his comedies.[3] As for Ninon he had himself carried to her house for the pleasure of

---

[1] For example, in " Plaintes du Carnaval," February, 1649 :—
> " Approche toy muse falote,
> Chère maistresse de Scarron,
> Qui n'aimes pas l'air fanfaron
> Dont se chantent les funérailles
> Des héros morts dans les batailles."

" Choix de Mazarinades," ed. C. Moreau. Paris, 1853, 2 vols. 8vo, vol. i. p. 268. *Cf.* " Bibliographie des Mazarinades," by the same, 1850, p. 206.

[2] " Reine, de qui j'ai tous les ans,
> Cinq cents écus beaux et pesans
> En bonne et loyale monnoie," &c.

" Œuvres Burlesques de M. Scarron." Paris, 1651, 4to, p. 75.

[3] " Dernières Œuvres," i. p. 23.

dining in company that recalled better days : "Je vous
en dirai davantage demain," he writes to the Marquis
de Villarceaux, "chez Mademoiselle de Lenclos, où je
me ferai porter à l'heure du dîner."[1] Ninon did not fail
to return the visits. Women of another stamp came
also ; among them no less a person than Madame de
Sévigné, to whom Scarron had written once, in his
happiest vein :—

"Madam, I lived abstemiously to the best of my
ability, in order to obey your command not to die
before you had seen me. But, madam, with all my
abstemiousness I feel each day I am dying of sheer
desire to see you. Could you not at least alter the
cause and means of my death? I should feel not a
little beholden to you. All these deaths from love
and longing are not natural to me, and are even less
to my liking. If I have mourned on a hundred
occasions people who died such deaths, think what
I should do in my own case, especially when I hoped
that I should die a natural death. But every one
must submit to fate. . . .

> "Et du moins souviens toi, cruelle,
> Si je meurs sans te voir,
> Que ce n'est pas ma faute.

---

[1] "Dernières Œuvres," i, pp. 22, 64.

" The rhyme is not very good, but at the hour of death we must think of dying, not of rhyming, well." [1]

Another very welcome guest of later years was Mignard the painter. Scarron had first met him in 1636 ; Mignard had since become famous : everybody at Court wanted to have his portrait painted by him, and the king had given the example. He had made at Avignon the acquaintance of Molière, then a strolling player of very inconsiderable fame, and had struck a friendship with him. This friendship resulted in Mignard painting his portrait, the best portrait extant of the master-dramatist, and in Molière writing his fine poem on " la Gloire du Val de Grâce," 1669, Mignard's most important work. As for Scarron he addressed copies of verses to " Monsieur Mignard, le plus grand peintre de notre siècle," and sometimes, using a more homely and not less pleasant style, he asked him to dinner, giving him in advance the following inviting menu :—"On Sunday, my friend, if you like, we shall have a good soup, followed by one or two ragoûts, a joint, dessert and cheese. We will drink some excellent wine ; a bright fire in my rooms will take off the edge of the cold. We will

---

[1] " Dernières Œuvres," i. p. 14.

have sweet wines, and compotes too with ambergris in them." [1]

We shall say nothing of the grandees and men of the world who came to Scarron's house, in order just to have been there, and because it was the fashion, and who choked the street with their carriages. "They flock," says Scarron, "to my rooms as people used formerly to flock and see the Elephant; they come here and spend the afternoon when they have missed their appointments and have nothing else to do." [2] To one of those grands seigneurs, this one a real friend, he playfully describes the state of his street when all the "carriage people" are away: "When you did me the honour to come and see me I prided myself very much upon it. Your carriage caused my little door to be venerated by every inhabitant of the Rue St. Louis, and more than one *porte cochère* envied its fate. The

---

[1] "Dimanche, Mignard, si tu veux,
   Nous mangerous un bon potage
   Suivi d'un ragoût ou de deux,
   De rôti, dessert et fromage ;
   Nous boirons d'un vin excellent,
   Et contre le froid violent
   Nous aurons grand feu dans ma chambre ;
   Nous aurons des vins de liqueur,
   Des compotes avec de l'ambre."
         "Dernières Œuvres," i. p. 251.

[2] *Ibid.*, p. 105.

du Rincy carriage alone maintains in my neighbours a feeling of awe, but they will lose it at last if some gentlemen of the Court do not come back soon to Paris and uphold till your return our somewhat shaky repute." [1]

II.—THE HUSBAND.

One day of the year 1650, when Scarron was in his apartment of the "Hôtel de Troyes," he received the visit of a person who could scarcely be described as a young lady and who was something more than a little girl. She wore a gown too short for her growth, and what with her gown, what with the peculiarities of the extraordinary being she was visiting, felt so much embarrassment that, not knowing what to say, she concealed her face in her hands and wept. Six months later, Scarron was writing to her : " Mademoiselle, I had always suspected that that little girl whom I saw six months ago, coming into my room, with too short a gown, and who began to weep, I scarcely know why, was as witty as she seemed to be. . . . But I should

---

[1] " Dernières Œuvres," i. pp. 69, 70. To Maréchal d'Albret, Oct. 13, 1659. The Rue St. Louis, now Rue de Turenne (corner of the Rue des Douze Portes, now Rue de Villehardouin), was the last place of abode of Scarron. His house still exists, almost untouched, and bears, according to M. de Boislisle's identification (*ut supra*, p. 66), the number 56.

never have imagined that either in the islands of America or at the convent of Niort the art of writing fine letters could be learnt ; and I do not understand for what reason you took as much trouble to conceal your wit as others take pains to display theirs." [1]

This young person of fourteen was the daughter of Constant d'Aubigné, himself the rebellious son of the famous Huguenot, Théodore Agrippa d'Aubigné, equally well known as a soldier and as a novelist, poet and historian. Constant d'Aubigné had obtained in 1645 a small appointment at Marie Galante, in the West Indies ; he went there with his wife and his children, Françoise (born at Niort in November, 1635) and Charles. He came back to France with his family in 1647, and died the same year. His wife found herself in complete penury. The three lived for awhile upon the alms of the Jesuits' college at La Rochelle : "the children came each in his turn every other day to receive at the door a dish of meat and potage." [2] Françoise, whose fate was to be more extraordinary than any heroine's in Scudéry's novels, was shortly after entrusted to the care of her wealthy and avaricious godmother, Madame de Neuillan, who tried to

[1] "Dernières Œuvres," i. p. 12.
[2] Geffroy, " Madame de Maintenon d'après sa correspondance." Paris, 1887, 2 vols. 8vo, p. 3.

persuade her out of her Protestant faith, and gave her as an occupation the keeping of turkeys. "I well remember," Françoise used to say many years later, "how my cousin and I, both of the same age, spent part of the day keeping my aunt's turkeys. They planted a mask on our noses to prevent the sun from burning our skin ; they set a small basket on our arm with our breakfast in it, and they gave us a little book containing Pibrac's quatrains, of which we had a few pages to learn every day. With this and a long pole in our hand we had to overlook the turkeys and prevent them going where they ought not." [1]

Such were the beginnings in life of one who was destined to marry the King of France, after she had been for eight years the wife of crippled Scarron. She was converted to the Catholic faith through the exer-

[1] Geffroy, "Madame de Maintenon d'après sa correspondance," p. 3. Madame de Neuillan's ideas as to the education of girls was destined to obtain the uncraved-for applause of worthy Gorgibus, who thus advises his daughter :—

> "De quolibets d'amour votre tête est remplie,
> Et vous parlez de Dieu bien moins que de Clélie.
> Jetez moi dans le feu tous ces méchants écrits
> Qui gâtent tous les jours tant de jeunes esprits ;
> Lisez moi comme il faut, au lieu de ces sornettes,
> Les quatrains de Pibrac. . . .
>   l'ouvrage est de valeur
> Et plein de beaux dictons à réciter par cœur."
>   "Sganarelle," by Molière, sc. 1, year 1660.

tions of the Ursulines at Niort, and then came with her
mother to Paris, where a common friend made her
acquainted with the poor poet.

Still hoping for his cure, Scarron had heard with
admiration of the wonders the climate of La
Martinique could work ; it was an averred fact that
M. de Poincy, who had arrived there disabled by
gout, now rode, fenced, and had recovered the complete use of his limbs. From that day Scarron only
dreamed of the West Indies, and gathered information
about them. A company had been established to
work the country round the Orinoco river ; he associated eagerly with it : " I have," he wrote to Sarrazin,
" taken a share of a thousand écus in the new company
of the Indies which is going to establish a colony three
degrees north of the equinoctial line, by the banks of
the Orellana and Orinoco rivers. Adieu France, adieu
Paris, adieu tigresses in angel plumage, adieu Ménages,
Sarrazins, and Marignys. I give up burlesque verses,
comical romances and comedies, to go to a country
where there will be neither false virtue, nor religious
cheats, inquisition, sharp winter, nor fluxions to smother
me, nor wars to famish me." [1]

His intention was soon known and created quite a
stir ; many deprecated his plan, verses were written about

[1] " Dernières Œuvres," i. p. 12.

it.　In his collection of epigrams [1] Furetière has the following : " So, that famous paralytic, who crawled along with many a moan, is starting on a journey to America, like Vespucci or Magellan?　He means to make discoveries, to people new harbours with merchants, scamps and navvies ?　I wish I may die if he is not setting about the most burlesque of all his works." [2]

---

[1] The first of which, called "La Feinte Rupture," is very pretty :—

> " Puisque tu veux que nous rompions
> Et reprenant chacun le nôtre
> De bonne foi nous nous rendions
> Ce que nous eûmes l'un de l'autre,
> Je veux avant tous mes bijoux
> Reprendre ces baisers si doux
> Que je te donnai à centaines ;
> Puis il ne tiendra pas à moi
> Que de ta part tu ne reprennes
> Tous ceux que j'ai reçus de toi.
> "Poésies Diverses," Paris, 1664, p. 77.

[2] " Donc ce fameux paralytique
> Qui ne marchait qu'avec ahan
> Va voyager en l'Amérique
> Comme Vespuce ou Magellan.
> Il veut faire des découvertes
> Et va peupler de nouveaux ports
> Avec marchands, gueux et manœuvres !
> Je meure s'il ne fait alors
> La plus burlesque de ses œuvres."
> Furetière, *ibid.*, p. 140.

This, " the most burlesque " of his undertakings, was not after all to be performed ; the journey, society, and project came to nothing mainly through the unexpected end of one of the originators of it, Abbé de Marivault, who, setting out from Paris to take ship at Havre, was drowned opposite the Cours-la-Reine.

The plan, however, had for Scarron some lasting consequence ; while busy with it he had become acquainted with Françoise d'Aubigné, " Bignette " as she was then familiarly called, and had been charmed with her wit, youth and beauty. Kindly as he was, he tried to place her at least above want, and offered either, if she were so inclined, to pay her *dot* to a convent, or, if she preferred, to marry her. This last alternative the young girl, who had kept no very pleasant remembrance of the Ursulines at Niort, decided to choose, and two years after the acquaintance was made, in April, 1652, [1] Françoise d'Aubigné's first marriage took place. She was then sixteen and Scarron forty-two.

This marriage proved very happy. Françoise tended the poor poet with great affection and care ; there is nothing but words of praise towards her in all Scarron's

[1] See various deeds concerning this marriage, discovered and printed for the first time by M. de Boislisle, " Paul Scarron et Françoise d'Aubigné," 1894, pp. 53 ff.

correspondence. She was full of tact as well as of wit, and in the most difficult and bizarre situation managed to keep her dignity, and even give some shade of it to the household itself.[1] She was not then the rigid, untractable woman of later years ; the rigours of the Convent des Ursulines still weighed upon her mind ; she did not dream yet of a repeal of the Edict of Nantes. With perfect feminine sense she knew what she ought to exclude and what she could endure, and was respected as well as admired. " She impressed," her relative Madame de Caylus wrote in her " Souvenirs," " everybody in such a way that no one in her presence durst utter a word of indelicate suggestion, and one of those young men said : ' If I had to take liberties either with the Queen or with Madame Scarron, I would not hesitate, I would rather take them with the Queen.' In Lent she would eat a herring at the end of the table and soon retire to her room." [2]

---

[1] Another lady, Céleste de Harville-Palaiseau, whom Scarron had for a while housed, after she had been cast off by a lover, had tried, not without some success, to reform the tone of the place. In a letter to her Scarron expresses his thanks for having been delivered through her exertions " des mauvaises compagnies," of which he says " j'étais accablé." But this reform was only temporary.—" Dernières Œuvres," i. p. 22.

[2] Ed. de Lescure, Paris, Janet, p. 44.

Whether or not there was some exaggeration
in this account, written long after, certain it is that
it was not Lent all the year round, and she did not
always retire so soon. The part she took in conversation delighted her husband, who, great connoisseur as
he was in those matters, was not long to see that few
could compete with his wife. He read his works to
her, and she attempted, not without some degree of
success, to get rid of what was too gross and licentious
in them. " Madame de Maintenon," we read in
"Segraisiana," [1] " who had no less wit than virtue,
was of great use to Scarron, for he consulted her about
his works and was much the better for her emenda-
tions."

Visitors became now more numerous than ever, and
more than ever was the street (first the Rue d'Enfer,
and later the Rue St. Louis, now Rue de Turenne in
the Marais quarter [2]) choked with carriages. " The
new bride," writes St. Simon, who is on other scores
extremely hard and unjust to her, " delighted the
different sort of people who called at Scarron's. He
saw the best and most varied society. It was the
fashion to visit him ; there came wits, men of the
Court, and men of the town ; he saw in his house the
best and the most distinguished people, upon whom he

---

[1] " Segraisiana," 1721, p. 114.   [2] See above, p. 86.

was unable to call himself, and who were ever drawn
to him by the charms of his mind, his learning, his
imagination, his matchless gaiety, which his sufferings
could never dull, and that gift of invention and that
jocosity which we still admire in his works." [1]

In all those gatherings Françoise d'Aubigné had her
word to say, be the subject of conversation literature
or philosophy, religion or travels.   We find her once
enlightening a great friend of the house, Segrais, the
collaborator of Madame de La Fayette, on those
curious things, little known at that time, pine-apples.
She remembered to have seen them at La Martinique,
and could vouch that they grew on a plant shaped like
an artichoke, and that the fruit had a taste " between
an apricot and a melon," [2] not at all a bad defini-
tion.

We see her also, when talkers grow unendurable,
leaving the house under pretence of paying visits to
her friends.   Scarron mentions good-humouredly her
goings out on these occasions as a sort of penance
inflicted upon him ; and he gives a pleasant insight
into his *ménage* when he writes in a kindly vein to his
friend Pellisson : " I am often surrounded with dunces
who pour upon me their silly jokes, their fun as frigid

[1]   " Mémoires," Chéruel's edition, Paris, 1873, vol. xii. p. 91.
[2]   " Segraisiana," p. 183.

as all the snows of the pole. My wife then leaves me to confront alone a danger which she ought to share with me ; she takes her muff and goes out to see some friend. But when I have good company, when you are here, or d'Elbene comes, or le Rinci, the lady behaves in another fashion." [1]

An amusing picture this of the young wife taking her muff and walking out in a pet when uncontrollable " mauvais plaisants " came, and of Scarron being left to mope. Among those who were sure not to make her look for her muff was Mignard, who, when he came back from Rome, found Scarron married and was a frequent guest during the last years of the poet's life. Long after, when the career of the artist was drawing to its close, Mignard painted for St. Cyr a portrait of " la Marquise de Maintenon," now in the Louvre. " He had known her in her youth," wrote Abbé de Monville, his biographer, " and found means to recall

[1] " Je suis souvent de sots environné,
    Mauvais plaisants plus froids que de la neige,
    Enfin plus froids que toute la Norvège.
    Ma femme alors me laisse en un danger
    Qu'elle devrait avec moi partager,
    Prend son manchon et va voir quelque amie ;
    Mais quand je suis en bonne compagnie,
    Toi par exemple, Elbene ou le Rincy,
    La dame alors n'en use pas ainsi."
                " Dernières Œuvres," i. p. 244.

her charms, without altering the expression age had given to her face." [1]

Another welcome visitor at the poet's home, and even for some time an inmate of it, was a certain mysterious friend who made Scarron and Françoise d'Aubigné acquainted, and who, after having taxed the ingenuity of all biographers, has just been identified by M. de Boislisle. He has left on the fly-leaves of a book now preserved in the National Library in Paris a long manuscript note of the greatest interest and importance for the history both of the poet and his wife and for the history of the poet's works. As it is not very accessible, and as there is not a word of it which does not convey some curious information, we here translate in full the part of it that concerns Scarron:

"The manuscript notes on the margins of this book were written by the Sieur de la Ménardière [2] who was

---

[1] See a reproduction of this picture in "The Comical Romance and other Tales by Paul Scarron," 1892, vol. i. p. xxii. A friendly portrait or description of Scarron and his wife is to be found in the great romance of Mlle. de Scudéry, "Clélie," where the two appear under the names of Scaurus and Lyriane.

[2] The book is called : "Apologie pour M. Duncan . . . contre le traité de la Mélancholie, tiré des Reflexions du Sr. de la Mre." 4to ; no date nor place. Press mark, Td. 86–14. Hippolyte Jules Pilet de la Ménardière, reader in ordinary to the king, member of the French Academy, and a physician of note, has left various works in verse and prose and some tragedies ; he died June 4, 1663.

private physician to the Marchioness de Sablé, received a salary from her, and lived at her house. Later on he became reader to the king. It is he who for some slight disease administered certain pills to M. Scarron (first husband of the Marchioness de Maintenon) which caused such a contraction of his muscles that, though he had been up to then a well-built, alert man, he became a cripple ; and his inability to use his limbs increased till his death.

" I knew Madame Scarron well, before she went to the West Indies. I saw her since at La Martinique, at her mother's, where I was lodging while our ship was being loaded, and afterwards at St. Christopher, at the house of the Commandeur de Poincy, where we remained two months. The mother had come to fetch her husband, the late M. d'Aubigné, son of the one who wrote the 'Universal History,' the 'Baron de Fœneste,' the 'Confession of Sancy,' and other works.

" I lived since for three years with M. and Madame Scarron, at the Hostel de Troyes, Rue d'Enfer, where they married in 1652. Madame d'Aubigné, the mother, had sent me a power of attorney [1] to represent her when the deeds for the marriage were drawn, and

---

[1] Printed for the first time by M. de Boislisle, " Paul Scarron et Françoise d'Aubigné," 1894, p. 53. It bears date February 19, 1652.

she wrote asking me to place her daughter in some convent till the time of the projected marriage. The young lady had been staying before that in Poitou with the Marchioness de Neuillan, to whose care she had been entrusted, and who came to stay at the Hostel de Troyes with her brother, M. Tiraqueau. There it was that the loves of the two began ; M. Scarron had apartments there, some of which were let by him to me. I boarded with him afterwards as well as Lafleur my servant, whom he often asked to make frangipane tarts in his presence.

"There again it was that he wrote, on my advice, the first volume of his ' Comical Romance ' dedicated to Cardinal de Retz, then coadjutor to the Archbishop of Paris, who often came to spend some pleasant hours with him, when he left the Luxembourg during the Fronde. I supplied him with the four Spanish tales, which he so cleverly translated, and inserted in his first two volumes, as well as with four others which he also translated and printed in a separate form. I suggested that he ought to give us a new translation of ' Don Quixote ' instead of the Ethics of Gassendi, which I found him busy translating. But he would not try, on account of a previous translation by Oudin and another, though that was very bad. I told him, if that was so, he had better begin some work of his own invention,

and conformable to his lively temper, rather than continue those Ethics of Gassendi, which were too serious
for him. I added that he should introduce some
novels, for which I would give him Spanish originals ;
I had many of them, and he knew the language. He
would thus imitate 'Don Quixote,' in the first part of
which four such pretty ones are to be found. So that
I may say that in a way the public owes me that
pleasant work (the 'Roman Comique'), though I am
not the author of it, and the four novels published
separately.

"I have some hundred charming letters which he
wrote me, and which I shall print some day if his
widow gives me leave. He wrote one among others
while I was at Sedan, beginning: 'What on earth are
you doing by the banks of the Meuse?'[1] in which he
bestows great praise on Marshal de Fabert, who, according to him, is not one of those marshals who are
led merely by instinct."[2]

The rest concerns only La Ménardière and his
quarrels with Duncan. There are many points in
this long note. We see that before she died Madame

[1] The hundred letters were not published, but this particular
one was printed among the "Dernières Œuvres" of Scarron.
The early editions (1663, 1668, 1696) do not contain it, but it is
to be found in the edition of 1709, p. 49.

[2] See below Appendix II.

d'Aubigné had had time to arrange for the marriage of her daughter with Scarron, and that she approved of it. We learn how Scarron, drawn once more by his taste for higher things, meant for a while to dedicate his leisure to the translation of Gassendi's works; and how at the request of his anonymous friend he consented to think of a lesser subject, which lesser subject turned out to be his " Roman Comique," the work by which he is specially remembered and which has long survived the faded fame of Gassendi's philosophy.

M. de Boislisle has placed beyond the possibility of a doubt who the author of this note was. We owe it to Esprit Cabart, Sieur de Villermont, a man of wit and learning who had travelled in many countries, and had been for a time Governor of Cayenne. Many years after the events here related, Madame Scarron, then the Marchioness de Maintenon, preserved a grateful remembrance of his kindness; and owing to her interference he could avoid some serious trouble which he had incurred by wearing unduly the titles of " Messire " and " Chevalier." [1]

III.—THE POET.

Among the various sources from which Scarron drew

[1] " Paul Scarron et Françoise d'Aubigné," 1894, pp. 39 ff.

his income were some pensions, one, not long continued,
from the Queen Mother, another from Surintendant
Fouquet, "the patron" as he constantly calls him, the
revenues (for a while) of his canonry at Le Mans, the
gifts following his dedications,[1] and the produce of
what he called his "Marquisate of Quinet."

Quinet was his publisher.[2] From his earliest days
Scarron had been known as a writer of easy, pleasant,
amusing verses. Such was their average character ;
they were apt, especially in after times, to sink into
scurrilousness, or (on rare occasions, it is true) to rise
almost to the level of Cornelian nobleness and grandeur.
"Little Scarron has always had an inclination towards
poetry," wrote Tallemant in his chapter on "Little
Scarron." His name first appeared in print as the
author of a copy of verses written in praise of Scudéry's "Lygdamon," one of the many plays drawn at
that time from D'Urfé's "Astrée," and performed in
1629. He wrote epistles, madrigals, epigrams by the
hundred ; they were handed round and greatly admired ;
many seem to have been lost, a large number remain.
Several collected editions of those fugitive pieces were

---

[1] Fifty pistoles, for example, from "la Grande Mademoiselle"
for his "Écolier de Salamanque" ; see "Segraisiana," 1721, p. 87.

[2] Quinet paid for Scarron's Virgil eleven thousand livres; see
Boislisle, p. 108.

given in Scarron's lifetime.[1] That mass of now forgotten poetry deserves to be better known, and the few
stray readers it now gets do not complain of the hours
spent in perusing it. Its particular merit consists in
what the poor author so sorely wanted in his body,
namely, agility ; the freedom of his demeanour as a
poet, the nimbleness of his movements, the alertness of
his gait are unparalleled. It seemed as if his mind had
profited in this respect with all that his body had lost.
His pleasure in being at least intellectually agile was so
great that he could refuse himself nothing ; sometimes
he is admirable for his elegance, more often he is
ludicrous for his gambols, japes, and mad pranks. "Why
would not my verse please even the queen ? " he wrote
in the dedication of his " Virgie," " as the meanest
monkey may sometimes amuse the most refined mind."
He was unsparing of his monkey tricks, and wry faces
were very frequent. Much more interesting and
curious will be some specimen of what he could do
when he meant to be graceful. There is much real
grace, and an exquisite harmony of words, in his
description of that fairy land, America, where at one

---

[1] For example : " Recueil de quelques vers burlesques," Paris,
1643, 4to ; " Recueil des Œuvres burlesques de M. Scarron . . .
dédiées à sa chienne." Paris, 1648, 4to ; second and third part,
1651 ; " La Relation véritable (ut supra) . . . et autres pièces
burlesques." Paris, 1648, 4to.

time he expected to travel, there to undergo a
new birth, as Faust was rejuvenated by his enchanted
beverage :

> "Il faut porter dans l'Amérique
> Un chagrin si mélancolique,
> Et voir si sous un autre ciel
> Son absinthe deviendra miel.
> Là nulle fluxion ni goute,
> Là nul froid que tant je redoute ;
> La nuit seulement un vent frais
> Y semble être fait tout exprès
> Contre le chaud de la journée ;
> Là le printemps toute l'année
> Y conserve sa gayeté,
> L'automne sa maturité,
> Et l'été, sans brûler les herbes,
> Chaque mois y donne des gerbes,
> Et tous deux des fruits ravissants,
> A la fois mûrs, nés et naissants." [1]

Another sort of merit to be noticed in Scarron's
poetry is his gift for close description from life. The
little he could now see he saw well ; he was an excellent observer of what was going on around him. Some
of his character sketches are so accurate and so full of
life that they would not be out of place in a comedy of
Molière. No *fâcheux* in Molière is better painted to
the life than a certain intruder who came one day to

---

[1] "Œuvres," 1786, vol. vii. p. 187.

bore poor Scarron, who could not escape. Every detail of the dress and speech is noted with a care and skill so perfect and accurate, the outline, colour, attitudes, and gestures so curiously observed, that nothing would be easier than for a painter to put the scene on canvas. Here it is complete :

" I was alone the other day in my little room, stretched on my bed, with pains in every limb, sad as mourning itself, sorrowful as one of the doomed race, cursing the day that I was born, when my little page, as silly as any in Frànce, came in and said : ' Mr. So-and-so wants to speak to you.' Though Mr. So-and-so was unknown to me, I could not help saying that he was welcome. And then, behold, there entered a eunuch face, with a gigantic periwig, which with both hands he tried to arrange ; he was all bespotted with red, yellow, and blue tassels ; his rhingrave was short, his legs were crooked. He wore *canons*, or rather rotundas, as large as any round table. He was humming, when he walked in, some old tune or other ; he leaned on his cane, giving himself great airs. After having curtsied to me with immense amplitude, his body swinging to and fro, he said with a smile and in a shrill voice : ' I am an admirer of your divine writings, sir, and for my part, sometimes I pride myself upon following you close in your comic vein. I come therefore to visit you as a brother author, and as being also your most humble servant.' " [1]

The *fâcheux* goes on undismayed, gives his opinion on Quinault, St. Amant, Furetière, " le docte Ménardière " (him of the pills mentioned above), on Corneille (" Corneille a fort baissé ") ; wants to know whether Scarron prefers " Clélie ou Cassandre," and what he is

[1] " J'étais seul l'autre jour dans ma petite chambre,
Couché sur mon grabat, souffrant en chaque membre,
Triste comme un grand deuil, chagrin comme un damné,
Pestant et maudissant le jour que je suis né :
Quand un petit laquais, le plus grand sot en France,
Me dit : Monsieur un tel vous demande audience.
Bien que Monsieur un tel ne me fût pas connu,
Je répondis pourtant : qu'il soit le bienvenu.
Alors je vis entrer un visage d'eunuque,
Rajustant à deux mains sa trop longue perruque,
Hérissé de galans rouges, jaunes et bleus ;
Sa rhingrave était courte et ses genoux cagneux,
Il avait deux canons ou plutôt deux rotondes
Dont le tour surpassait celui des tables rondes ;
Il chantait en entrant je ne sais quel vieux air,
S'appuyant d'une canne et marchait du bel air.
Après avoir fourni sa vaste révérence,
Se balançant le corps avecque violence,
Il me dit en fausset et faisant un souris :
Je suis l'admirateur de vos divins écrits,
Monsieur, et de ma part quelquefois je me pique,
De vous suivre de près dans le style comique.
Je vous rends donc visite en qualité d'auteur
Et de plus comme étant votre humble serviteur."
   " Épitre chagrine ou Satire III., Œuvres," vi. p. 175.

working at just now. " Will you not finish your pretty romance?"

> " N'achèverez vous point votre joli roman ? "

and so on for pages.

The main basis of Scarron's repute as a writer of verse was, however, in his time, his two burlesque poems, " Le Typhon," published in 1644,[1] and " Le Virgile travesti," the first two books of which were printed by Toussaint Quinet, in 1648.[2] This last work appeared under the patronage of the Queen Mother; the first had been dedicated to Mazarin, and had for its subject the epic quarrel of the Giants and the Gods :

" I sing the horrid Typhon, him of the hooked nose, like a griffin's, who had only two shoulders, but one hundred arms as long as poles, . . . who was so bitter-minded that I am at times ashamed of him. I sing also those gentlemen his brothers, who were not far behind him when the business was to uproot a mountain, to cross a bridgeless river, to flatten the highest peak to the level of the plain, pull up great pine-trees and use

---

[1] " Typhon ou la Gigantomachie, poème burlesque, dédié à l'éminentissime Cardinal Mazarin." Paris, 1644, 4to ; frontispiece by H. David. Mazarin took no notice of the dedication, and this incited Scarron not a little to side with the Frondeurs.

[2] " Le Virgile travesty en vers burlesques." Paris, 1648, 4to. Curious engravings.

them as sticks, and yet they found them rather short ; and with the same gave a drubbing to many a god who never mentioned it." [1]

The title of the work is well justified. There is something prodigious, gigantic, enormous in all the doings of Scarron's heroes. They are grotesque, no doubt, but still enormous ; they would have made friends with young Gargantua and invited him to sit and play on their knees. Being very hungry one day they espy oxen at the plough ; they devour them without taking the trouble to "pluck off the ploughs." They play at skittles on a certain Sunday to while away the time, their skittles are long pieces of rock,

[1] " Je chante l'horrible Typhon
Au nez crochu comme un griffon,
A qui cent bras longs come gaule
Sortaient de deux seules épaules . . .
Au reste d'esprit si quinteux
Que j'en suis quelquefois honteux.
Je chante aussi messieurs ses frères,
Qui certes ne le lui cédaient guères,
Tant à déraciner les monts
Qu'à passer rivières sans ponts,
Mettre les plus hautes montagnes
Au niveau des plates campagnes
Et des grands pins faire bâtons
Qui n'étaient encore assez longs,
Desquels maints grands coups ils donnèrent
A maints dieux qui ne s'en vantèrent."

they get warm in their play and throw their stone playthings about; one falls on the foot of Typhon, who in his rage picks up the skittles and sends them all—to the gods.

> " Il ramassa quilles et boules
> Et les jeta sans regarder
> Tant que son bras les put darder.
> Les quilles d'un tel bras ruées
> Passèrent bientôt les nuées,
> Et perçant la voûte des cieux
> Donnèrent jusqu'où tous les dieux
> Humaient sans songer à malice
> L'exhalaison d'un sacrifice,
> Et de nectar se remplissaient
> Que les déesses leur versaient,
> Résolus de boire et reboire
> Pour le moins jusqu'à la nuit noire."

One of the skittles falls on the cupboard and breaks all the crockery. Jupiter, who slept, "having taken one glass too much," jumps to his feet crying : "I say, what is the matter?" ("Dites donc, qu'est-ce qu'il y a?") No one dares answer except Cypris, who carelessly says, "Oh! nothing," and is rebuked with words we shall not reproduce. Jupiter soon gets at the truth, and understands it must be war. Mercury is ordered away the better to ascertain facts, and his flight to Helicon is described with that particular agility of verse which was one of Scarron's gifts : "Having tied

wings to his heels, over fields, over towns, he flew
light as a falcon, straight towards Helicon, to see the
nine sisters, refresh himself and drink at the spring.
He found the nine learned ones, seated on benches,
busy dissecting roundels, sonnets, and stanzas, on
sorrows, on partings, on favours won. . . ." [1]
They were in fact, it seems, anticipating our friend
Bourget's psychology and analysis. A terrible war
is waged, with uncertain success for a while ; at last
Typhon is vanquished and shut up under Mount Etna.

> " Et moi je mets fin à mon conte
> Tiré du sieur Noel le Comte." [2]

Such literature of course could not please Boileau ;
he could not allow without a protest " les filles de

[1] " Puis ayant mis ses talonnières . . .
Par dessus champs, par dessus villes,
Vola léger comme un faucon
Droit vers la montagne Hélicon,
Pour voir les filles de mémoire
Et là se rafraichir et boire.
Il trouva le docte troupeau,
Les neuf savantes demoiselles,
Assises dessus des bancelles,
Qui faisaient dissection
De rondeaux, de sonnets, de stances,
Sur des chagrins, sur des absences,
Et sur des plaisirs accordés."

[2] Otherwise Noel Conti or Natalis Comes, an Italian writer of
the sixteenth century.

mémoire" to be thus derided ; he wanted them, we may suppose, to keep their voices clear to sing with him of "Namur." He is therefore loud in his condemnation of "Typhon," which, with one contemptuous line, he exiles from Paris to the provinces.[1] "Typhon" none the less enjoyed a considerable degree of popularity, and its success encouraged Scarron to attempt more in this line ; it caused in fact the poet to write his huge " Virgile travesti."

This, too, was a success, and even a more marked one than his former work. For us this vast compilation is past enduring : the joke is too protracted ; witticisms, clever tricks, happy thoughts, curious japes, gambols, and grimaces abound, but they last too long, they are too numerous ; we soon get to know the utmost the "monkey" can do, and want to push the door open and get out into the fresh air. "Typhon" has at least this merit, that it is comparatively short. But seventeenth century people took in such works a

---

[1] "Au mépris du bon sens, le Burlesque effronté
　　Trompa les yeux d'abord, plut par sa nouveauté. . . .
　　Mais de ce style enfin la cour désabusée
　　Dédaigna de ses vers l'extravagance aisée,
　　Distingua le naïf du plat et du bouffon
　　Et laissa la province admirer le Typhon.
　　Que ce style jamais ne souille votre ouvrage."
　　　　　　　　　　　　　"Art Poétique," i.

particular pleasure for a cause which no longer exists : they had at times a surfeit of dignity, etiquette, and periwigs, and this made them enjoy grins, tricks, and bald pates. We know what was the tone of conversation in Scarron's rooms, and we know too that St. Simon described it as " la plaisanterie du meilleur goût " ; one must be very tired of Versailles to say so. Racine read the " Virgile " with laughter and delight, not unaware that he was sinning against the gods and Boileau, but somehow feeling that his was a pardonable sin. There is not a shade of vituperation or scorn in the letter where Madame de Sévigné informs her daughter of what books she has taken to while away the time in her journey from Paris to Grignan, books not many copies of which are now sold to ladies at railway stalls : " We found no reading worthy of us, but Virgil, not in travesty, I say, but in all the majesty of the Latin and Italian."[1] On account of those contrary tastes mentioned before, people were then able to admire Virgil in his majesty and in his travesty too. Poussin did not, but he was an exception.

The success of the " Virgile " was extraordinary ; it pleased the queen; it delighted Chancelier Séguier, so much so that, hearing of his approval, Scarron dedicated his second book to him ; it had a number of editions

[1] Madame de Grignan, July 16, 1672.

and was found not unworthy of the Elzevir press ; it caused at last such a flood of " burlesque " poems that even Scarron felt sick of it, and expressed the hope that the French Academy, then in its early youth, would interfere : " Perhaps the wits who have been enlisted to keep our tongue pure from all taint will see to it. . . . As for me I am quite willing and ready to give up a way of writing which has spoiled so many."[1] He wrote two books more after this offer, and then stopped of his own accord, not waiting for an injunction from the Academy.

IV.—THE DRAMATIST.

" I scarcely write anything now, but comedy verses," Scarron said once to a friend ; " for I draw from them most of what I get." He had always been fond, as we know, of plays and players, and when nothing was left him but his clear mind, instead of following actors from tennis-court to tennis-court, he wrote for them.

His first comedy, " Jodelet ou le Maître valet," performed in 1645 at the Marais theatre, enjoyed great popularity. The famous actor Jodelet, who gave to the

[1] *Dédicace* of Book V. to Councillor Payen Deslandes, 1650. The work was finished by Moreau, Seigneur de Brasei. As for Scarron's innumerable rivals and imitators in the burlesque style, see Victor Fournel's edition of the " Virgile Travesti," introduction, and p. 189.

play his own "nom de théâtre,"[1] was at his best when he appeared in it ; his queer look and ugly face, his large mouth, his speaking through the nose were the more ludicrous, as he had to act under silk and ribbons the part of his own master, Don Juan. He was destined to be some years later one of the original actors in Molière's " Précieuses," where he appeared as " le Vicomte de Jodelet," while Molière himself was Mascarille.

At the date when Scarron's first play was performed Molière was twenty-three, and had as yet written nothing ; Racine was a child of six, but Corneille, who was Scarron's elder by four years, had already produced his most famous dramas, and, without speaking of his tragedies, had put on the stage his comedies of " Le Menteur" (1642) and "La Suite du Menteur" (1643), in which Jodelet had had a great success as Cliton. Both plays were adapted from Spanish originals, for Spain was in this respect what France has been of late : the great storehouse where dramatists of many countries came for their plots, and sometimes for their wit. Her authors were numerous and prolific, and their

---

[1] Instead of taking it from the play as M. Fournier wrongly asserts (" Théâtre complet de Scarron." Paris, 1879, 8vo, p. xiii.). This actor was known as "Jodelet" when he performed Corneille's " Menteur" (1642) : "Le héros de la farce, un certain Jodelet . . . " (" Suite de Menteur," i. 3).

8

repute as inventors of adventures, unexpected rencontres, grand discussions on noble matters, farcical characters, was so well established that most foreign dramatists and novelists called at their stalls and supplied themselves freely. We owe to Spain " Le Cid " as well as " Le Menteur," and the bulk of Scarron's dramatic works : most of the latter are drawn from Calderon and Rojas. Scarron asked his friends to send him Spanish comedies, as he would have asked them for any other commodity ; he was very indignant at the thought that people about town spoke Spanish less purely than in former days, and heard once with pleasure that there was a renewed demand for grammars :—" The sale of Spanish grammars has not reached fifty thousand livres, as you say, but we are not far from that number. The Spanish tongue has never been so corrupt as it has been of late in Paris. I am much beholden to you for the trouble you take in seeking Spanish comedies for me." [1]

After " Jodelet ou le Maître Valet " Scarron wrote a number of comedies or tragi-comedies, the principal of which are " Jodelet duelliste," performed in 1646 (under the name of " Les trois Dorotées ") ; " l'Héritier ridicule," 1649 ; " Don Japhet d'Arménie," 1652 ; " l'Écolier de Salamanque," 1654 ; " Le Marquis

[1] " Dernières Œuvres," i. p. 62.

ridicule," 1655, or beginning of 1656;—the plot of them all being laid in Spain, in Madrid, Toledo, Orgas, or Valencia.

In these plays Scarron appears with his usual qualities of ease and alertness, his gift for observing attitudes and noting curious details, his irrepressible gaiety, and that strange combination of tastes that made him relish tragic grandeur as well as farcical buffoonery. Whenever there is an opportunity for using a higher style Scarron never lets it pass. If he has not the genius he has at least a taste for proud heroes and grand scenes. The thought of Corneille is constantly upon him ; Corneille was, with Malherbe, the master he recognised, the true god of his literary religion. In more than one scene of " Jodelet on le Maître Valet," Don Juan speaks the language of the Cid ; he is, in fact, nothing else than a Cid caught in a comedy, as may happen any day to any Cid in real life. The thing is so visible that Scarron has it noticed by the very persons in his play.[1] But Scarron sometimes overdid what he

---

[1] Jodelet to Don Fernand :—

   " Que vous eussiez aimé pour votre gendre un Cid
   Qui vous eût assommé, puis épousé Chimène ! " (iv. 5).

Cf. in " L'Écolier de Salamanque" the part of the Count; see for example his speeches to old Don Felix :—

   " Tes injures, tes cris ne peuvent m'irriter ;
   Je veux un ennemi qui puisse résister.

attempted, and his debates between passion and duty, in
"l'Écolier de Salamanque," for example, inspired as
they are by the Cid's, are too superhuman. The danger
of striving after Corneille is that one reaches Scudéry.

Lesser people in Scarron's theatre are remarkable for
their clear outline and their life-like expression; he
looked at men with the eye of a draughtsman. Few
series of plays better lend themselves to be illustrated,
few are less difficult to put on the stage; though there
are almost no stage directions, words adapt themselves
to situations so well that there is an attitude under
each, and no actor with any gift could miss it.

The details of actual life are introduced with a care
and accuracy very rare on the French stage of the
time; people drop their spectacles, want to know the
hour, tell stories, feel cold, take notice of and suffer

> Je ne veux point de femme et quand j'en voudrais une,
> J'en choisirais une autre et d'une autre fortune.
> Pour me la faire prendre il fallait me prier,
> Non pas me quereller, non pas m'injurier.
> Je ne fais rien par force et fais tout par prière ;
> Aux humbles je suis doux ; aux fiers j'ai l'âme fière ! . . .
> Don Felix.   Ah ! si ton bras m'épargne, insolent ravisseur,
> Je préfère tes coups à ta fausse douceur . . .
> Viens, viens finir mes jours, ils n'ont que trop duré." [&c]
>   ii. 1.

It is obvious that Scarron remembered the scene in the "Cid,"
i. 3 and 4.

from a number of trifles which mere puppets would
not attend to : " Do read, please, for I have lost my
spectacles and I do not know where to find others fitting
my sight."

> " Lisez donc, aussi bien j'ai perdu mes lunettes,
> Et n'ai pas trop aisé d'en retrouver de nettes,"

says old Don Fernand, " Hang the bolt which has
caught my fingers ! "

> " Maudit soit le verrou qui m'a pincé les doigts ! "

exclaims Beatrix.   At another place she thus describes
Jodelet, who, unknown to everybody and under a
disguise, has to pay court to Isabelle, while the real
Don Juan acts as his servant : " Your son-in-law is
there, beautiful to look at, new varnished, new shaven,
well-powdered, curled, and trimmed, laughing as a
madman, besprinkled with jewels like a Chinese
king."

> " Votre gendre est là-bas, beau, poli, frais tondu,
> Poudré, frisé, paré, riant comme un perdu,
> Et couvert de bijoux comme un roi de la Chine."

Both are betrayed by their attitude and language,
and Isabelle is sure to love for life the man she could
not help loving even while passing as a valet.   The
same plot has been turned to account by Marivaux in
his delightful " Jeu de l'Amour et du Hasard."

In "l'Écolier de Salamanque" Crispin pays his court to a lady's maid in a most proper and approved fashion: " Beatrix, darling, let us have some scandal now, and give freedom to our tongues; tell me all about thy mistress and I shall tell thee all about my master. Let us talk about our gains, or tell stories ; let us say all the good things we remember. I must tell thee a tale. There was once a king. That king lived in a wood. In the midst of that wood . . ." [1]

All these plays are in verse—Scarron's easy-going verse, verse with no pretension, adapting itself to circumstances, a light verse and sometimes intentionally faulty. He will on occasion, instead of looking for a proper rhyme, coin a new word to suit a line and tease his reader ; once he manages to have *Beatrix* rhyme with *larme*, straining the words thus :

> " Or, si vous en tirez la moindre lacrimule,
> Je vous donne gagné, foi de Béatricule.

---

[1] " Béatrix ma mignonne,
Médisons un moment sans respecter personne ;
Médis de ta maîtresse et moi je te dirai
Du maître que je sers tout ce que je saurai.
Parlons de nos profits, contons nous des histoires,
Exerçons à l'envi nos heureuses mémoires.
Je veux t'en conter une. Il était une fois
Un roi. Ce roi faisait sa demeure en un bois ;
Au milieu de ce bois. . . ." [&c. &c.] iii. 3.

Vous riez, Don Louis, de ce diminutif ?
Dame, nous en usons, et du superlatif.
Un certain jeune auteur, qui tâche de me plaire,
Quand je vais visiter mon cousin le libraire,
M'apprend tous ces grands mots ! " [1]

And if we do not consider this enough, and still
object to "lacrimule," a quantity of explanations are
yet in store, and the poet will go on for ever till we
bow acceptance. This trick and many others Scarron
has in common with a very different sort of a poet,
whose name, unlikely as it may seem, often recurs to
the mind when reading the poor cripple's works : I
mean no less a person than Alfred de Musset. The
bent and aim of the works of both are as different as
can be ; but they sometimes resemble each other in
their peculiarities and details. Musset, too, is very
fond of volunteering explanations for avoidable mistakes, which he prefers not to avoid; [2] he has the
same eye for neat picturesque outlines, for amusing
sketches, the same taste for deriding silly pomposity.
Secondary resemblances these, but resemblances all the
same. Scarron besides was well known to Musset.

Irus' way of appreciating the merits of his servants
in " A quoi rêvent les Jeunes Filles " reminds us of
Don Japhet's own attendants.

[1] " Jodelet ou le Maître Valet," iii. 2.
[2] There are a number of such cases in " Namouna," where,

"Spadille a l'air d'une oie et Quinola d'un cuistre"

is becoming proverbial, as Don Japhet's lines have long been :

> "Don Zapata Pascal,
> Ou Pascal Zapata, car il n'importe guère
> Que Pascal soit devant ou Pascal soit derrière."

-----

besides, a passage in Scarron is introduced in full. Scarron's verses :—

> "Nous voila tous sur le pavé ;
> Sur mon dos mon père élevé
> Nous éclairait de sa lanterne . . .
> Ma Créuse venait derrière . . .
> Au vieil temple nous arrivâmes . . .
> Quasi tous, car ma femme hélas . . .
> Se trouva manquer à la bande . . .
> Mon père ne fit autre chose
> Que me dire : 'Elle reviendra
> Ou bien quelqu'un la retiendra ;
> N'est elle point resté derrière
> Pour raccommoder sa jartière ?'"

("Virgile Travesti," ii. Fournel's edition; Paris, Garnier, pp. 119, 120) become in Musset :—

> "Je suis comme Énéas portant son père Anchise.
> Énéas s'essoufflait et marchait à grands pas.
> Sa femme à chaque instant demeurait en arrière.
> 'Créuse, disait-il, pourquoi ne viens tu pas ?'
> Créuse répondait : 'Je mets ma jarretière,'" &c.
>
> "Namouna," i. 75, 76.

The scene is represented in a curious engraving in Scarron's first edition.

There is in Musset a number of such comical encounters as the one between Don Japhet and the Bailli.

—" Bailli, votre fortune est grande,
Puisque vous m'avez plu.
    —Le bon Dieu vous le rende ! "

" Don Japhet " is the most famous, as it was the most successful, of Scarron's plays. There is more drollery in it than in any other of his comedies. Don Japhet, who is the fool of Emperor Charles Quint and claims distant kinship with his master,

" L'empereur Charles Quint, ce héros redoutable,
Mon cousin un deux mil huitantième degré,"

comes to Consuegra in search of a wife. He is welcomed by the Commander in the same fashion as Don Quixote and Sancho are welcomed by the Duchess. All sorts of practical jokes are played upon him, but his cowardice and pomposity prevent him from retaliating. He is beaten and derided ; a number of ridiculous accidents mar an appointment he had or thought he had with his betrothed. At last, in the same manner as M. Jourdain was to become " mamamouchi," he resolves to marry a Peruvian infanta answering to the beautiful name of Ahihua, and concerning whom a letter from the great Mango Capac to his cousin Japhet is publicly read : " Let her be the wife of Japhet my cousin. I give to both the produce of a tax I have lately laid upon flame-coloured parrots and upon the lamentins of the great river Orellana." [1]

No better sort of income had poor Scarron himself derived from the great river Orellana, where he had dreamed of going to make a plantation.

When " Don Japhet " was published it appeared with a dedication to King Louis XIV., a free-spoken one in which Scarron says : " I shall only try to persuade your Majesty that it would not hurt you much to do me a little good. If you did me a little good, I should be merrier than I am, I should write funnier comedies ; your Majesty would be better amused ; and if you were better amused your money would not prove ill-spent."

The pleasure young Louis had taken at the adventures of Don Japhet had been very keen indeed ; his taste for that play lasted all his life. Fifty years later, when Scarron had long been dead and his young wife had become old Madame de Maintenon, the Great King had still " Don Japhet " performed

---

[1] " De mon cousin Japhet qu'elle soit l'épousée ;
Je leur donne un impôt que j'ai mis depuis peu
Tant sur les perroquets qui sont couleur de feu
Que sur les lamentins du grand fleuve Orillane."

before him at Fontainebleau and Versailles (1703).
He has been often reproached with his dislike for the
" magots de Teniers " ; many excuses could be found
for his aversion to those gloomy, pale-faced drunkards.
Certain it is that, with all his dignity and wigs and
ribbons, he was a man and a Frenchman, and enjoyed
his laugh as much as any. Most of Molière's farcical
comedies were first performed before him, " George
Dandin " in 1668, " Pourceaugnac " in 1669, " Bourgeois Gentilhomme " in 1670, &c., and their success
had been great at court before the Paris public had
a chance to say its say about them.

Scarron's plays enjoyed for the same reason no small
degree of favour, both at court and in town. For a
long while they were constantly on the bill of Molière's
troupe. They did not always bring much money, but
neither did always Corneille's tragedies. We find, for
example, in Lagrange's " Registre " of the troupe under
the year 1659 the following entries :—

April 30.—" Jodelet Maître Valet " ... 155 livres.
May 3.—" Cinna " ... ... 175 ,,
May 7.—Performed at Vincennes, " Don Japhet,"
    for the king.
Aug. 1.—" L'Héritier Ridicule " .... 130 ,, [1]

[1] " Registre de Lagrange, 1658–1685, publié par la Comédie
française," Paris, 1876, 4to.

These three plays of Scarron recur from time to time with various success, bringing sometimes 226 livres and sometimes only 96. But it must be remembered that Corneille's "Cid" could be played (July 11th) for 100 livres, and his "Rodogune" (July 3) for 42. All those numbers show by comparison what was the run when there was a new play by Molière himself. The first performance of the "Précieuses" brings to the troupe 523 livres, the second 1,400, the third 1,004, and so on, and the troupe is asked by great people to give private performances in their houses. "Les Précieuses" are thus performed at the houses of Michel le Tellier, of Chevalier de Grammont, of La Maréchale de l'Hospital, &c. The cardinal and the king want also to see the new play, and Lagrange makes in his journal the following entry :—"Oct. 26, 1660. 'L'Etourdi' and 'Les Précieuses' at the Louvre, in the apartments of his Eminence Cardinal Mazarin, who was ill in his chair. The king saw the comedy, standing incognito, and leaning on the back of the chair of his Eminence." In November the king asks for "Don Japhet," and again the following year. In June, 1663, "l'École des Femmes" and "La Critique de l'École des Femmes" are performed together, bringing 1,357, 1,130, 1,355, 1,426, 1,000, 1,357, 1,731 livres, and so on. We are very far from the 42 livres for "Rodogune" and

96 for "Don Japhet," which none the less continued to be performed from year to year by the troupe.

They have now long ceased ("Don Japhet" alone excepted) to appear on theatrical bills and deserve perhaps a better fate. Their construction, no doubt, is loose, their conclusions are patched up and do not fit very well ; the innermost coils of the human brain and heart are left alone for future psychologists to unroll them. There are only sketches in these plays ; but they are pleasant sketches, drawn with a clever hand, guided by an observing eye, such sketches as Scarron's contemporary, Abraham Bosse, was wont to draw and engrave. Collectors and *curieux* consider them well worth the preserving.

V.—The Novelist.

When Scarron became a novelist, he did not cease to busy himself with players. They were his particular delight ; he took them for the subject of his principal tale. Nor did he cease to think of Spain and to look to Spanish authors for his originals. We have seen his friend, Cabart de Villermont, supplying him with Spanish novels " of which he had a number." He published separately a small collection of tales adapted from Spanish authors in which there is plenty of love and adventures, masks, swords, and tokens ; much fancy and good grace, sweet discussions under balconies and behind lattices, long veils concealing the prettiest faces in the world, prancing horses, valorous cavaliers, Andalusian eyes such as those which were to shine and sparkle again in literature during that second advent of Spanish heroes to France, when Hernani paced the stage, and Don Paez fell in love with the Lady Juana.

Scarron's novels enjoyed a great success, and were often reprinted in the seventeenth and eighteenth centuries ; they numbered among their readers Molière, who took several hints from them. One or two passages in " Tartuffe " have a striking resemblance with some lines in Scarron's tale, " Les Hypocrites." When there is a first attempt at unmasking the " faux-dévot " Montufar, the rabble, who have been entirely taken by the hypocrite's sweet demeanour, rush at the accuser, and want to kill him. But Montufar interferes in his favour, and exclaims : " I am the wicked one . . . I am the sinner, I am the one who never did anything acceptable to God. Do you think . . . because you see me dressed as a pious man should be, that I have not been, all my life long, a thief, a cause of scandal to others, and my own perdition ? You are mistaken, my brethren ; hurl at me your insults and stones ; draw upon me your swords.—With this he ran towards his foe and threw himself at his feet." [1]

Finding himself in a similar situation, and accused by Damis, the son of the house, Tartuffe addresses Orgon thus : "Yes, my brother, I am a wicked one, a guilty one, a sinner," &c.

> " Oui, mon frère, je suis un méchant, un coupable,
>   Un malheureux pécheur tout plein d'iniquité,
>   Le plus grand scélérat qui jamais ait été.
>   Chaque instant de ma vie est chargé de souillures ;
>   Elle n'est qu'un amas de crimes et d'ordures. . . .
>   [*Addressing Damis.*]
>   Oui, mon cher fils, parlez, traitez moi de perfide,
>   D'infame, de perdu, de voleur, d'homicide,
>   Accablez moi de noms encor plus détestés,
>   Je n'y contredis point, je les ai mérités
>   Et j'en veux à genoux souffrir l'ignominie." [2]

Though Montufar is not less severely punished at the end than Tartuffe himself, it must be confessed that the morality of Scarron's novels is very lax indeed. Scenes of an unedifying character abound ; from the

---

[1] "Je suis le méchant . . . je suis le pécheur, je suis celui qui n'ai jamais rien fait d'agréable aux yeux de Dieu. Pensez vous . . . parce que vous me voyez vêtu en homme de bien, que je n'aie pas été toute ma vie un larron, le scandale des autres et la perdition de moi même ? Vous vous êtes trompés, mes frères ; faites de moi le but de vos injures et de vos pierres et tirez sur moi vos épées.— Après avoir dit ces paroles . . . il s'alla jeter . . . aux pieds de son ennemi." [2] iii. 6.

moral point of view those tales are not commendable, and we do not commend them.

Not contented with his collection of " nouvelles tragi-comiques," Scarron, following upon the example of Cervantes and encouraged by his friend Cabart, interspersed his " Roman Comique " with short Spanish tales,[1] very pleasant in their way, which have this advantage among others, that they show the difference between fancy pictures and real life : for if " l'amante invisible " is well painted, Destin and l'Étoile are not painted at all ; they are flesh and blood.

We have seen under what circumstances the idea was suggested to Scarron of writing " quelque ouvrage de son chef." Cabart had found him engaged on a translation of Gassendi's ethics, a philosophical taste Scarron had in common with Molière, who had

---

[1] The originals of each have been pointed out by M. Fournel ; the three first are taken from Solorzano's collection of novels called " Los Alivios de Cassandra " ; the fourth, from the ninth tale in the " Novelas Exemplares " of Maria de Zayas. (" Roman Comique," Paris, 1857, introduction, pp. lxxv. *et seq.*) Scarron has been supposed to have taken the idea of his " Roman Comique " from Rojas' " Viage Entretenido " or the " Amusing Journey " ; but the only resemblance is that both deal with strolling players ; Scarron needed no Rojas to suggest strolling players, and he owes more to Filandre's troupe than to Rojas' inventions for the making of his novel. (As to Filandre, see *infra*, p. 133.)

attended in his youth Gassendi's lectures in the house of Chapelle, the father. Scarron dropped his translation to follow the advice he had received ; and very good advice it proved, for it made him write the first tale of real life, studied from nature, which can be inscribed on the list of modern French novels.

Many, of course, had been the attempts. It is almost impossible to say, with literal truth, of any variety of literary work that at this or that date it *began ;* critical minds will always object and quote a number of names ; in this case without going further back than the early part of the century they will name d'Aubigné's " Baron de Fœneste," 1617, Théophile de Viau's " Fragments d'Histoire comique," written about 1620, Charles Sorel's "Francion," 1662, and many others. Long lists of them are to be found everywhere ;[1] we shall not add one to the number. " But," as Burke once observed wisely enough, " though no man can draw a stroke between the confines of day and night, yet light and darkness are upon the whole clearly distinguishable." In the same manner when we follow the history of the novel we come step by step to the place where Scarron stands ; critics if so minded will be able to show that there is no immense gap between each step,

[1] For example, in Victor Fournel's introduction to his edition of the " Roman Comique," Paris, 1857.

that there are plenty of country scenes in " Francion,"
and plenty of real life in " Baron de Fœneste." The
impartial reader will for all that keep the impression
that all those works were merely attempts, and that with
Scarron he has something better.

He has something very much better indeed. You
may open the book almost at random and feel it at
once, so much real air, true sunshine and life there is in
it. Any few lines of the novel will transport the reader
to some pleasant part of old provincial France. He
will make a stay there, if he has any feeling for French
white roads and green rivers, with old castles and
young poplars, for the close-shorn meadows with their
herds of dreaming cows, and for the noisy little rivulets.
The Loire country, where we are transferred, especially
deserves a visit ; it is more characteristically French
than any other, and stands foremost in literature. It
saw in former years the romantic adventures of divine
Astrée and matchless Celadon ; it saw again and again
Rabelais' heroes on their way to Paris, to Thélème or
to Chinon, " ville fameuse, voire première du monde " ;
it is just now the place where Scarron's strolling players
love and quarrel, and play Corneille.

Do you like such places and such people ? Have
you any fondness for roadside adventures, for talkative
ostlers, for laughing maids, their laughter as an echo of the

larks' song in the morning ; for paths lined with hedges
and leading to a green unknown somewhere? And if
you like all this, will you not like it the more if, in the
middle of the scenery of to-day, for it has not altered,
you meet people of a former time, as truly alive and
young as the very sun above us ; poets who knew M.
de Corneille, players on their way to Paris, a medley of
artists, mountebanks, and runaway scholars bewitched
out of Sorbonne by this or that stage deity? Turn
the page, and here begins the " Comical Romance,"
which proved in its time the delectation of the Court
and town—the Court of the Grand Roi, the town of
Molière.

In his account of comedians [1] Tallemant des Réaux
has a word to say of provincial troupes, then very
numerous. But he names only two by name, for most
of the troupes that *did* the Seine, Loire, or Garonne
regions had rarely a continued personal life ; they
collected and dispersed, vanished and reappeared. The
two he names are, for different reasons, remarkable.
Concerning one of them, he says : " I must end with
the Béjart. I have never seen her on the stage, but I
am told she is the best actress of all.[2] She belongs to

[1] " Historiettes," ed. Monmerqué and P. Paris. Paris, 1857,
6 vols. 8vo, " Historiette " CDXXXVI.

[2] She was something of a playwright and adapted plays. We
see in the " Registre de Lagrange," p. 300, that the troupe plays,

a provincial company. . . . A fellow called Molière left the benches of the Sorbonne to follow her ; he was long in love with her ; he used to give hints to the company ; then he became a member of it. . . . He has written plays with wit in them. He is not a very good actor except in comic parts. His plays are performed only by his own company ; they are comedies."

The "fellow called Molière," who wrote plays which *were* comedies, led for fifteen years or so the life Destin and l'Étoile live in Scarron's novel. The troupe to which he belonged associated in 1643, and the contract is still in existence. While the tennis-court "des métayers" was being prepared in Paris for their accommodation, "l'Illustre Théâtre," as they called themselves, went first to Rouen, and some time after made their *début* in Paris, a very unpromising one, which only brought debt, ruin, and prison to Molière. They resolved to leave town again, and then began for the dramatist the thirteen long years of his apprenticeship, during which he travelled the provinces and was seen at Nantes, Toulouse, Narbonne, Agen, Montpellier, Lyons, Pezenas, Béziers, Avignon (where he met Mignard), Dijon, Grenoble,

January 30, 1660, "Don Quichot ou les Enchantements de Merlin, pièce raccommodée par Mlle Béjart." The performance brings 300 livres.

and a number of other places. They were known after 1647 under the title of " troupe des comédiens de M. le Duc d'Épernon," and their reputation was great in the provinces. Scarron was well aware of it ; he makes Destin say at the beginning of his novel, " our troupe is as complete as that of the Prince of Orange or of His Grace the Duke of Épernon ; " and it has been often asserted that he had Molière's troupe in view in his " Comical Romance." But it is not so. In his remarkable work, " La troupe du Roman Comique dévoilée," [1] Henri Chardon has demonstrated that another company of players was in his mind.

We have said that Tallemant des Réaux mentions two. Concerning the second he writes briefly : " There is in another company a man called Filandre, who has also got a reputation, but I do not think him true to nature." This Filandre, whose real name was Jean Baptiste, Sieur de Monchaingre, was, according to Chardon's very plausible argument, the prototype of Scarron's Léandre, and his wife sat as Angélique, whose name she bore. They retired later to Anjou, where they had become landed proprietors of some importance, and there died respectively in 1691 and 1695. For many and many years they had, before that time, moved from town to town in the provinces,

[1] Le Mans, 1876, 8vo.

leading exactly the same life as Molière ; and several members of their troupe were destined to be connected in various ways with the great dramatist's. Thus Filandre's company included a " petit Guérin," who was to become in future years the second husband of Molière's wife. Thus again an adopted daughter of Filandre, a cast-off child of Dutch origin, became enamoured of Jean Pitel, the candle-snuffer of the same troupe, married him about 1664, got a reputation under the name of Mademoiselle Beauval,[1] and by order of the king had to leave the province and join Molière's company at Paris.[2] She made her *début*,

---

[1] See her portrait and the portrait of her husband in Hille-macher, "Galerie historique des Portraits des Comédiens de la Troupe de Molière." Lyon, 1869, 8vo, pp. 107 and 113.

[2] This order, a very curious and characteristic one, reads like an anticipation of the famous " Moscow decree." It runs thus : "De par le Roi ! Sa Majesté voulant toujours entretenir les troupes de ses comédiens complètes, et pour cet effet prendre les meilleurs des provinces pour son divertissement, et étant informée que la nommée Beauval, l'une des actrices de la troupe des comédiens qui est présentement à Macon a toutes les qualités requises pour mériter une place dans la troupe de ses comédiens qui représente dans la salle de son Palais Royal, mande et ordonne à ladite Beauval et à son mari, de se rendre incessamment à la suite de sa cour pour y recevoir ses ordres. . . ." Her associates are ordered to let her go " nonobstant toutes conventions, contrats et traités avec clauses de dédit . . . attendu qu'il s'agit de la satisfaction et du service de Sa Majesté. . . . Fait à St. Germain en Laye, le xxxi. Juillet, 1670." Signed, " Louis," and further below, " Colbert." Chardon, p. 91.

two months later, before Louis, as Nicole of the
"Bourgeois Gentilhomme." Her little daughter Louise
was the Louison of the "Malade Imaginaire," in which
piece her husband played the part of Diafoirus.

Such was the company which visited the Mans
country at the time when Scarron was there, and which
he had in his mind while writing. Of such sort were
his heroes, men and women of flesh and blood, with
feelings of their own, with wit and foibles. He is
fond of them, and describes their outward appearance,
their dress and attitudes, the tone of their voice, with
something of a Chaucerian care ; many of the inmates
of the inn at Le Mans would not have disfigured the
table of mine host of " The Tabard." The eye Scarron
had for details and picturesqueness never exercised
itself with better effect. His old man totters on,
" carrying a bass viol on his shoulders ; and because he
stooped a little as he went, one might have taken him
at a distance for a great tortoise walking upon his hind
feet. Some critic or other will perhaps find fault with
the comparison, by reason of the disproportion between
that creature and a man ; but I speak of those great
tortoises that are to be found in the Indies ; and besides, I make bold to use the simile upon my own
authority." [1] Destin, " as poor in clothes as rich in

---

[1] " Comical Romance," Lawrence and Bullen, 1892, i. p. 4.

mien, walked by the side of the cart : he had a great patch on his face (which covered one of his eyes and half of one cheek), and carried a long birding-piece on his shoulder, wherewith he had murdered several magpies, jays, and crows, which being strung together made him a sort of bandoleer ; at the bottom of which hung a hen and goose, that looked as if they had been taken from the enemy by way of plunder. Instead of a hat he wore a night-cap tied about his head with garters of several colours. . . . His doublet was a griset-coat . . ." &c., &c.[1]

Scarron pays the attention good painters do to hands and feet ; his heroes stand or lean, we always know how ; their hands hang down or carry something, we are informed of the what and the wherefore. Destin bows " without offering to pull off his turban, because with one hand he held his gun and with the other the hilt of his sword, lest it should knock against his legs." Little Ragotin, big Madame Bouvillon, lean la Rappinière, the curate of Domfront, stand in full light with every particular of their dress and figure so visible that it seems as if we should recognise them in the street.

More art even is spent with the actresses ; they are scarcely described at all, and we feel and know, without the possibility of hesitation, how pretty and modest

[1] " Comical Romance," Lawrence and Bullen, 1892, i. p. 4.

they are, how elegant in their dress and witty in their speech. Even when there is scarcely a word about them, we enjoy the charm of their presence.

In his novel (much better than in his plays) Scarron busies himself with something more than the externals of his heroes ; I mean with their thoughts and subtler feelings. Of course he does not launch into long disquisitions about their sentiments ; psychological literature was not to his taste, though largely practised in his day, according to the fashion of the time, in heroical romances. But he knows how to give in a few brief words a just impression of the temper and qualities of his not very complicated heroes. They are plain, straightforward men who go their way, and laugh at downhearted people ; they even laugh at the poet of their own troupe, who is in love " with one of the two she-players; but, however, he was so discreet, though a little crack-brained, that it was not yet discovered which of the two he designed to wheedle into compliance with the fair hope of making her immortal." There is much knowledge of the human heart displayed in the one brief sentence, in which Scarron describes the state of mind of Destin when he has lost his love (for a while), and says : " Je pleurai comme un enfant et *je m'ennuyai partout où je ne fus pas seul.*" In another single sentence Scarron summarises much of the psychology of provincial life in all times : " La ville du Mans se trouva pleine de chasseurs que le bruit de cette grande fête attira, la plupart avec leurs femmes, qui furent ravies de voir des dames de la cour *pour en pouvoir parler le reste de leurs jours auprès de leur feu.*" Don Carlos falls in love with a lady whom he has heard speak, but never seen : " tant l'esprit a de pouvoir sur ceux qui en ont." [1]

Many other such examples, showing insight into the human heart and a knowledge of human nature, might be adduced ; for many are the occasions on which our heroes' tempers are put to the trial, and they have to display whatever there is in them of courage or cowardice, love or hate. Scarron's aim in his novel was to oppose all sort of exaggerations, all *invraisemblances*, all magnifying of people or sentiments ; he meant in all seriousness to paint from life. He did not pretend to lead his heroes, but he was, on the contrary, led by them : " One chapter brings on another," he said, " and I do in my book as those who let the reins loose, and allow their horses to do as they please."

From the few extracts just given it will have been already gathered that one of Scarron's main attractions

[1] I. Chapters 1 and 9.

consists in his style. While in most of the writers of
fiction in his day style was either too high or too low,
constantly verging on pomposity or vulgarity, his own
has a sobriety and directness combined with such a
happiness of expression as to stand unsurpassed when
he is at his best. With all his jocosity and fun he
knows how to be tender and delicate ; his language
being quite natural, with no " parti-pris " of any sort,
fits with perfect flexibility events and circumstances.
He is not the man to blow with Scudéry his own
trumpet ; he does not sing of " le vainqueur des
vainqueurs de la terre " ; sometimes, however, he
sings, and sometimes he murmurs, and sometimes he
laughs, he sneezes, and even barks. His style remains
in keeping with his theme ; it adapts itself equally to
Mlle. de la Boissière's adventures and to Ragotin's
misfortunes. He coins words, barbarisms we should
call them in other authors ; but he resumes so quickly
his well-behaved attitude, that we have no time to
grumble ; and truly they are not lapses, but skips of
his pen. Who would have the heart to blame Ragotin
and his " figure *oursine* " ; who would refuse himself
the pleasure of seeing the crust of the pasty served to
the Bohemians being eaten by the black little *bohémillons*
their children, or disagree with the statement that we
live in a time when everybody " se *marquise* de soi
même " ?

Sharp, short sayings, witty or weighty, abound in his novel. Ragotin was " assez mauvais poète pour être étouffé s'il y avait de la police dans le royaume ; " La Rancune, " qui s'était altéré à force de boire, ne faisait que remplir les deux verres ; " the Curate of Domfront, " fit consulter sa gravelle par les médecins du Mans, qui lui dirent en latin fort élégant qu'il avait la gravelle (ce que le pauvre homme ne savait que trop) et ayant aussi achevé d'autres affaires . . . il partit de l'hôtellerie." Destin, while in Italy, and very poor : " était assez bien vêtu, comme il est nécessaire de l'être à ceux de qui la condition ne peut faire excuser un méchant habit."

In one single sentence little scenes are brought before our eyes, the persons, their attitudes, their feelings ; scenes that might tempt the pencil of a draughtsman. While journeying on his donkey, Ragotin is persuaded by La Rancune to spout verses from Théophile's tragedy of " Pyrame et Thisbé " : [1] " Certain peasants who attended a loaded cart, and were going the same way, hearing him speak with the emphasis of an enthusiast, thought he must surely be

---

[1] The famous tragedy from which Boileau picked out, to be pilloried for ever, the two ridiculous lines :—
> " Voici donc le poignard qui du sang de son maître
> S'est souillé lâchement. Il en rougit le traître ! "

preaching the word of the Lord ; and therefore, as long as he rehearsed his heroics, they walked cap in hand by his side and respected him as an itinerant preacher."[1]

In the "Comical Romance" the adventures are many. Life was then much more adventurous than it is now, and Scarron could put many incidents in his novel which look extraordinary to-day. Everything that happens in his story did happen, or might have happened to Filandre's or to Molière's troupe. A number of small details scattered here and there in his work will help the reader to realise the difference of the times ; and for this reason the novel has an historical as well as a literary value. Take an example, a trifling one : very often while travelling in the East you are informed of your coming near an inhabited place by the smell of decaying carcases of beasts (the scavenger-dogs not having completed their task). Such was the state of things in the France of the Grand Roi, and we find in Chapter XIV. a horse that had been killed allowed to remain on the spot and be eaten by dogs and wolves.

There is a double current of adventures in Scarron's

[1] "Quelques paysans qui accompagnaient une charrette chargée et qui faisaient le même chemin crurent qu'il prêchait la parole de Dieu, le voyant déclamer là comme un forcené ; tandis qu'il récita, ils eurent toujours la tête nue, et le respectèrent comme un prédicateur de grands chemins " (II. ch. 2).

novel, each serving as a set-off to the other. There are the comparatively elegant adventures of Destin, L'Étoile, Léandre, and Angélique, and the gross adventures of La Rancune, La Rappinière, and Ragotin; these last very gross indeed, and if very comical at times, at others very unsavoury. These are the only parts of the novel which remind us unpleasantly of the sick-room where it was composed. It seems very curious now how greatly they were relished in those times, and how such grossness could be reputed " plaisanterie du meilleur goût," to use St. Simon's word. Scarron's visitors, those even of the best sort, greatly encouraged him in it; he used to read to them chapters of his novel, and when they laughed he would say : " 'Tis all right, the book will be a success." " I remember," writes Segrais, " that I went once to see him, with Abbé Franquetot. ' Take a seat,' said he, ' and stay here, that I may *try* my "Comical Romance" upon you.' And at the same time he took a few sheets of his work and read some of it. When he saw that we were laughing : ' Good,' said he, ' the book will do, as I see it makes such clever people as you are laugh.' He thereupon accepted our congratulations. He called this trying his Romance, in the same way as a coat is tried on. He was funny and amusing in everything." [1]

[1] " Segraisiana," 1721, p. 142.

But something more than incitements to a laughter of no refined quality came from Scarron's sick-room. Higher topics than night adventures in the obscure corridors of country inns were discussed in that apartment where the wits of the time used to meet. Many of those discussions are reproduced by Scarron in his book, who describes men of his day, and is careful always to place them in their proper frame and *milieu.* The literary problems which then troubled the minds and had not been solved yet—for a time—by grave Boileau, dramatic questions especially, constantly recur in his pages. The merits and demerits of the famous unities, the Spanish drama, the liberties of the old French stage of which Ragotin appallingly avails himself in his "Faits et gestes de Charlemagne en vingt journées," the antiquated examples left by Garnier and Hardy, the rendering of plays by good and bad players at the Hôtel de Bourgogne, the Marais or in the provinces, the talents of the dramatists Tristan, Théophile, and Mairet, the unparalleled genius of Corneille—such and many others are the questions over which they fight or agree when they are enjoying their rest at the inn or at some country Mæcenas' house.

No other book gives a better idea of the fire and sincerity with which literary theories were at that time attacked or defended ; it must be remembered that we are still on the threshold of the reign, at a time when nothing had yet been settled. It was not so long since the Academy had passed its sentence on the " Cid," and such an effervescence continued as was only once witnessed since—I mean in 1830, when the fight was renewed over the Cid of new-born times, that other Spaniard, Hernani.

Scarron himself was never tired of extolling Corneille. Of all his plays "Nicomède" is the one Scarron prefers, because it is so dignified : " On représenta le jour suivant le ' Nicomède' de l'inimitable M. de Corneille. Cette comédie est admirable à mon jugement, et celle de cet excellent poète de théâtre en laquelle il a plus mis du sien et a plus fait paraître la fécondité et la grandeur de son génie, donnant à tous les acteurs des caractères fiers, tous différents les uns des autres." Molière, who created so many Sganarelles and Scapins, and excelled in personating them on the stage, far preferred to play emperors : Scarron, even while writing of Typhon, and sitting squat in his wood and iron arm-chair, dreamed of yet unbuilt Versailles.

While his pet adoration was Corneille, his pet aversion was the long-drawn heroical novel as it was then understood; his raillery of any such is frequent and amusing, and much more to the point than Boileau's. The heroical novel was just then reaching the height of its prosperity ; the Hôtel de Rambouillet was in its glory, and Magdeleine de Scudéry was publishing amidst unparalleled applause her "Clélie," with the "carte du tendre" in it, the first volume having been printed in 1649, the tenth and last to be issued in 1654. "I cannot positively tell," says Scarron, alluding to the heroes of such novels, "whether he had supped at this time or whether he went to bed without a supper. Neither do I care to imitate the writers of romances, who mark with great exactness all the hours of the day, and make their heroes rise betimes, relate their adventures by dinner-time, eat but little at dinner, then resume the story after dinner, or retire into the thickest part of a wood, in order to entertain themselves, unless they have something to say to the rocks and trees. At supper-time they make them repair at the usual hour to the place where they eat ; there they sigh and look pensive instead of eating ; and thence go to build castles in the air on some terrace-walk that looks towards the sea, whilst the trusty squire reveals that his master is such a one, son to such a king ; that he is the best prince alive, and though he be still the handsomest of all mortals, that he was quite another man before love had disfigured him." [1] The publish-

[1] The "Comical Romance," 1892, i. p. 36.

ing of Scarron's "Roman Comique" did, however, more than his raillery or jokes towards destroying the hold such novels had on the readers.

The first part of his novel appeared in 1651 [1] with an engraved title-page, representing a stage with Italian maskers on it ; it was dedicated to Retz : "Au coadjuteur, c'est tout dire " ; the second part was published in 1657 ; the work was left unfinished. Several sequences and conclusions have been added ; the best known being the one edited by Offray, a Lyons publisher and a contemporary of Scarron.

One of the main defects of Scarron's novel, as such, is shown by the fact that it could as well have been left as it was. His book presents to us a succession of scenes full of variety and life, but it has no particular aim and leads to nowhere, or rather it so obviously leads from the very first page to the nuptial altar where Destin and l'Étoile, Léandre and Angélique

[1] A copy of the very rare first edition is preserved at the Arsenal Library in Paris, where is to be found also the best collection (though an incomplete one) of the original editions of Scarron's works : "Le Romant Comique de M. Scarron," Paris, Toussainct Quinet, 1651, 8vo. The title-page bears the motto of Quinet : "Heureux Quinaist ainsi." The "Achevé d'imprimer " runs thus : "Achevé d'imprimer pour la première fois, le 15 jour de Septembre, 1651." The engraved frontispiece bears date 1652. The last chapter in the volume is the twenty-third and last of the first part.

will join hands, to live happy together for ever and ever with plenty of children around them, that we have very little curiosity further to hear of what we already know. Scarron was well aware of this defect, and with his usual want of literary hypocrisy he did not make the faintest attempt at concealing it. He wrote scenes as they occurred to him with no more of a preconceived plan than can be put to the credit of Sterne himself,[1] leading his lovers and traitors and chance comers here and there along the roads and across country ; they follow " chemins creux," they make their escape at night and travel on horseback, telling their adventures till morning comes. Players as they are they behave themselves very well ; if there is much grossness there is no indecency. In this Scarron greatly differs from such novelists as Smollett, whose grossness thoroughly equals our author's, and is not relieved by the very enjoyable charm and good behaviour of the heroes in the " Comical Romance."

[1] Some of his scenes, depicted with a particular attention to attitudes, gestures, and physiognomy, are well worth comparing with Sterne, to whom Scarron was undoubtedly familiar. See, for example, the scene between Ragotin, Father Gifflot, and the nuns, part ii. chap. xvi.

VI.—Scarron's Fame.

Scarron survived the publication of his unfinished novel three years. He often alludes to it in his letters and his verses, and declares that he means to continue it,[1] but time passed on and the year 1660 came, when he sank and died. His main regret was for his wife, to whom he was more attached than ever. " The last time that I saw Scarron," writes Segrais, " as I was taking leave of him before my journey to Bordeaux, he said, ' I shall die soon, I know it : my only regret will be to leave my wife in want.[2] Her merits cannot be too much extolled, and I cannot sufficiently express my gratitude towards her.' "[3]

---

[1] " Ma santé [m'a] obligé à venir prendre l'air à une lieue de Paris, où j'espère achever une comédie et la conclusion de mon Roman." To Fouquet. (" Dernières Œuvres.")

[2] He left her in absolute want ; see an account of his debts (including the unpaid bills of the butcher, tailor, apothecary, &c.) in Boislisle, p. 97. Their house had, however, always been well and pleasantly furnished. See the " Inventaire fait à la mort de Scarron," *ibid.*, p. 183.

[3] In the deed by which a royal pension was awarded to her in 1666, mention was made, as a motive, of her husband's "services." See, in the MS. Clairembault, 1165, fol. 162 (National Library, Paris) the note concerning the " Brevet d'une pension de 2,700 livres accordé par le Roy le 23 fevrier 1666 à la dame Françoise d'Aubigné, veuve du feu Sr. Scarron, tant en considération des services dudit Scarron qu'en considération de ceux du feu Sr. d'Aubigné ayeul de ladite dame."

When Segrais came back from his "voyage de Bordeaux" he hastened to the house of his friend; but it was too late. "When I came to his door I saw that they were removing the chair upon which he was always seated and which had just been sold at auction. That was an arm-chair, with iron arms that could be pulled forward, and which supported a table for him to write upon or eat off." [1]

He was buried in the church St. Gervais,[2] where, says Théophile Gautier, "his tomb, as I think, is still to be seen." I went some time ago to ascertain; it is *not* to be seen. The church is paved with large flagstones, nearly all of them covering a tomb. When the *calorifère* was built a number of them were removed and a skeleton was found in almost every instance. Most of them bear now no inscription or have been so

---

[1] "Segraisiana," 1721, pp. 114 and 133.

[2] He had written for himself the following epitaph, marked by his usual resignation and good humour :—

> "Celui qui ci maintenant dort
> Fit plus de pitié que d'envie
> Et souffrit mille fois la mort
> Avant que de perdre la vie.
>
> Passants, ne faites pas de bruit
> Et gardez vous qu'il ne s'éveille,
> Car voici la première nuit
> Que le pauvre Scarron sommeille."

defaced as to baffle all inquiry; none remains with the name of Scarron. A low wainscoted chapel with paintings on wood is traditionally called Scarron's chapel, and the beadle will tell you that Madame de Maintenon used to come here and mourn for her first husband. But this is merely a catchpenny saying, and there is not a particle of truth in it. The only tomb of note to be seen above ground is the large white and black marble sarcophagus of Michel le Tellier, whose "oraison funèbre" Bossuet delivered in this same church twenty-five years after Scarron's death.

Even in his lifetime Scarron's fame as an author had been very great. Different as it was from everything that had been seen before, and especially from the heroical novels which were then the fashion, his "Roman Comique" enjoyed an immense popularity. It pleased the Court as well as the town. Young Louis XIV. is suspected to have read it, "en cachette." Mazarin was very wroth at the discovery: "The Cardinal," writes Madame de Motteville, "coming one day into the room where the king was in bed on account of some slight illness, saw my brother, who was reading something to amuse his Majesty, Scarron's Romance, maybe. He was greatly shocked and blamed this as if it had been a great crime." [1]

[1] Year 1657. "Mémoires," Paris, 1878, vol. iv. pp. 89, 90.

Such men as Fouquet and Condé read it and were
delighted. "Have some care of me," Scarron wrote to
his patron the "surintendant," "for, if I were to die,
you would have no more of those romances which
made you laugh so, no more Don Japhet, which amused
the king so much, no more verses, no more prose, no
more Scarron : in a word, of all those no mores the
last is the worst, for when you are dead, were it only
for a minute, then dead you are for ever and ever." [1]
As for Condé, the news of his having such a reader
delights Scarron : "Is it really possible that the Grand
Condé knows that I am alive ? My friend Guenault
tells me that he has seen the second part of my ' Roman
Comique' on his table. I am very proud of that." [2]
In fact Scarron's heroes soon became as well known as
those in "Astrée"; they too were quoted as being
familiar to everybody. Madame de Sévigné, writing
from Grignan, thus describes the coming home of
her son-in-law with a bruised face : " Il était tombé

---

[1] "Alors, plus de romans qui vous firent tant rire,
Et plus de Dons Japhet qui plurent tant au roi,
Plus de vers, plus de prose, en un mot plus de moi.
De tous ces plus, le dernier est le pire,
Car s'il faut qu'on soit mort un instant seulement,
On est mort éternellement."
"Dernières Œuvres," i. p. 231.

[2] "Dernières Œuvres," i. p. 66.

à Sorgues sur un degré et s'était tellement cassé le nez et un peu la tête et avait de si grands emplâtres que jamais la Rappinière ni le Destin n'en portèrent de plus remarquables."[1] In another letter the charming l'Étoile comes in for a comparison.

No one of course pleases everybody, and some "esprits chagrins" protested against Scarron's fame. Michel Bégon for one, who was making a collection of portraits of the illustrious men of his century, wrote to Cabart de Villermont in 1689 that he doubted whether he would have the portrait of Scarron, adding, however, that he considered Molière a better man, though according to him the difference between the two was not great. No higher praise than this would-be blame has ever been bestowed upon Scarron. "I have got the works of Scarron," wrote Bégon ; "I have not his portrait ; but I am not quite sure I shall give him place in my collection : I do not much like his *badinage*. Molière is, I consider, a better man, though neither must be ranked among the illustrious of our time." [2]

The success of the novel induced no less a man than La Fontaine to draw a comedy from it. Good La Fontaine had a particular knack of constructing detest-

[1] Oct. 14, 1694.
[2] "Michel Bégon, Correspondance et Documents inédits," ed. Duplessis, Paris, 1874, p. 24.

able plays from excellent novels. His "Ragotin," which he wrote in collaboration with Champmeslé, was represented on the 21st of April, 1684. It was performed only for ten nights; the characters in it are overdrawn; caricature has invaded all the play, the dramatist is even more unpardonably ferocious than Scarron had been towards poor little Ragotin, nothing is left of the charm of Angélique and l'Étoile. Some years later, not made wiser by this failure, La Fontaine busied himself with "l'Astrée," and had an operatic play on this subject performed in November, 1691. All he got for his pains was to be served with such epigrams as the following :—

> "On ne peut trop plaindre la peine
> De l'infortuné Céladon,
> Qui, sortant des eaux du Lignon,
> Vint se noyer dans la Fontaine."

Another attempt at paying Scarron literary honours did not prove more successful. In 1733 his novel was turned into French verse—not, however, into poetry —by le Tellier d'Orvilliers, who followed as closely as could be his original, so closely, indeed, that a strong flavour of prose entirely pervades his poem.[1]

[1] "Le Roman Comique mis en vers." Begins thus :
> "Monsieur Phébus allant bon train,
> Etoit plus d'à moitié chemin
> Et son char penchant vers le monde,
> Roulloit en s'approchant de l'onde."

It was translated into several languages, and more than once into English. One of the English translations was made by Tom Brown and various collaborators (1700), and another by Goldsmith. In a third and earlier one we find clumsy attempts at an adaptation. The name of London is substituted for Paris; "France" becomes "England"; when the poet of the troupe prides himself upon a personal acquaintance with Corneille and Rotrou, the English translator adds Shakespeare to the list: "And above all the rest, the poet, with a ring of admirers about him of the chiefest wits of the town, was tearing his throat with telling them he had seen Shakespeare, Ben Jonson, Fletcher, Corneille; had drunk many a quart with Saint Amant, Davenant, Shirley, and Beys; and lost good friends by the death of Rotrou, Denham, and Cowly."[1]

Better than anything else, the success the "Roman Comique" enjoyed with draughtsmen and engravers testified to its vitality. Without speaking of the collection of pictures by Coulon now preserved in the Museum at Le Mans,[2] and of the cuts adorning various

---

[1] "Scarron's comical romance : or a facetious history of a company of strowling stage players, interwoven with divers choice novels, rare adventures, and amorous intrigues . . . by the famous and witty poet, Scarron." London, 1676.

[2] They had been painted to order, to adorn a room in the castle of La Vernie. Coulon, who belonged to the Mans country,

Watteau pinxit.

E. Leroux Sculpsit sup.

Arrivée des Comédiens dans la ville du Mans.

Tome premier chap. 1er.

A Paris chez L. Larÿue rue des Noyers vis à vis la rue des Anglais place St Roy.

old editions, it was twice taken as the subject for a series of large plates by famous artists in the eighteenth century. The well-known " animalier " Oudry, who had not yet won his repute in this capacity, nor painted the numerous royal or ducal dogs now in the Louvre and elsewhere, made about 1717–1719 a very fine series of drawings, full of life and of a sort of Hogarthian humour, which were separately engraved and published. A number of them were engraved by himself. The famous Pater, in conjunction with Dumont, published another series between the years 1729 and 1739. There is more grace in them than in Oudry's work, but less life. The series by Pater and Dumont has been republished in our time by Anatole de Montaiglon,[1] and we give a reduced facsimile of the first plate in the original collection. Oudry's illustrations, or rather a choice of them, have been reproduced in Lawrence and Bullen's English edition of the " Comical Romance," 1892.

Of late years, as the taste for novels has gone on increasing, Scarron's fame has kept pace. Fine editions and cheap editions of his " Roman " have greatly mul-

painted them in 1712–16 in a very vulgar style, bordering on caricature, but with great spirit.

[1] " Le Roman Comique de Scarron, peint par J. B. Pater et J. Dumont le Romain." Paris, 1883, fol.

tiplied. Paul Bourget published one, Anatole France another; Zier illustrated a third. Victor Fournel gave an annotated text in Janet's " Collection Elzévirienne." The best critics of our time have busied themselves with him. He has been honoured with a biography by Guizot,[1] with a chapter by Théophile Gautier,[2] with quotations by Alfred de Musset.

Gautier took from him the hint for his " Capitaine Fracasse," mixing, however, in it many new elements, some drawn from Sorel, some from Walter Scott (the siege of the castle, for example, which had obviously the same architect as Torquilstone), some from his own fund. Among the latter we must mention the place allotted to landscape descriptions, which are as numerous and prolix in " Fracasse " as they are brief and scant in Scarron. The mere description of Sigognac's ruinous château occupies sixteen pages ; and when we have finished reading it we may well wonder whether we see it better before our eyes than the Mans country, with its hedges and poplars and " chemins creux," of which so little is said but to such good purpose in Scarron. And turning back to that curious mine which we have so often used, the " Segraisiana," we feel after this experience well prepared to subscribe to

[1] In his " Corneille et son Temps."
[2] In his " Grotesques."

Madame de La Fayette's wise saying as to how "une période retranchée d'un ouvrage vaut un louis d'or et un mot vingt sols."

Of late years a very clever book was devoted to Scarron and his works by M. Morillot, and important articles of great biographical interest were published, as we have seen, in the " Revue des Questions historiques " by M. de Boislisle.

Of all the honours conferred upon Scarron after his death, the most unexpected was the striking of a medal in his honour. " Par mesdames les neuf muses," he had written once, " je n'ai jamais espéré que ma tête devint l'original d'une médaille." But it did. It was engraved by Curé, and represents, on one side, Scarron's face, and on the other an emblematic scene with the appropriate motto :

" J'ai vaincu la douleur par les ris et les jeux."

IV.

A JOURNEY TO ENGLAND IN THE YEAR 1663.

I.—THE TRAVELLER INTRODUCED.

AMONG the familiars of the French Embassy, in the year 1663, when the Comte de Cominges represented the Grand Monarch at the British Court, was a strange person, who belonged partly to the Church and partly to the world, a Protestant by birth and a Catholic by trade, named Samuel Sorbières, or de Sorbières, as he preferred to be called. He was travelling in England to see the sights, to improve his knowledge, and to become better acquainted with the famous philosopher, Thomas Hobbes, of Malmesbury.

Sorbières was then between forty and forty-five years of age ; he was born at St. Ambroise, in the diocese of Uzez ; his father, his uncle (the then well-known Petit), all his family were staunch Protestants ; and so

Cernitur in vultu probitas, candorque, fidesque:
In scriptis reliquas perspice mentis opes.

Joannes Maury

PORTRAIT OF SORBIÈRES, BY N. BONNART, 1664.

was Sorbières himself, to all appearance, during many years. He lived for a while at Paris, then in Holland, then at Orange, where he was appointed principal of the local college. His easy manners, easy speech, easy style in writing made him an agreeable correspondent and companion, and he became, early in life, acquainted with several of the best men of the day ; he exchanged letters with Gassendi, Father Marsenne, Hobbes, Saumaize. A number of epistles addressed by him to Saumaize are preserved in the National Library, Paris (MS. Fr. 3930); they treat of learned questions ; they contain copies of recently discovered inscriptions ; they are full of friendly assurances and respectful compliments to both Mr. and Madame de Saumaize.

Sorbières had while young studied theology ; then medicine ; then he had devoted himself wholly to the making of his fortune, for the improvement of which he allowed himself to be converted in good time to the Catholic faith. " I have heard," Guy Patin writes in 1653, " that our old friend, M. Sorbières, master of the college at Orange, has proved a turn-coat, and has become a Roman Catholic. He was requested to do so by the Bishop of Vaison, and by the Cardinals de Bichi and Barberin . . . Of such kind are the miracles which can be witnessed to-day—miracles, I say, of the political and economical, rather than the metaphysical order. He is a widower[1] and a clever fellow, but, sharp as he is, I wonder whether with that new shirt of his, he will succeed in making his fortune at Rome, for the place swarms with hungry and thirsty people."

The thirst and hunger of Sorbières were of the keenest, and he took immense pains to assuage both; he journeyed to Rome, appealed to the king, wrote against the Protestants ; but his want of character was against him ; he only got temporary favours, small allowances, and unimportant livings. He did his best from year to year to ingratiate himself with cardinal, king, and pope ; he never failed nor succeeded entirely. From Mazarin he got little ; from Louis XIV. he received the empty title of Historiographer Royal (1660) and, what was more to the purpose, a pension of a thousand livres ; from Clement IX. he obtained a trifling gratuity, given once for all, and many kind words. His *déboire* on this last occasion was great : "They give lace cuffs," he said, "to a man without a shirt !" As his disappointment lasted long he had time to circulate this consolatory witticism, to improve it and remodel it ; several of the " variantes " such as : "I wish they would send me bread for the

---

[1] Sorbières had married, while in Holland, a Frenchwoman called Judith Renaud ; they had a son, Henry, who, after the death of his father, caused a part of his papers to be published.

butter they kindly provided me with," have been
preserved by his friend Graverol.[1]

Before his journey to England, Sorbières was known
to literary men principally by his translations. He had
turned from Latin into French Sir Thomas More's
" Utopia," Hobbes's " De Cive," Bates's " Elenchus
motuum nuperorum in Anglia."[2] He had also written
a few essays, letters and discourses, on philosophical,
medical, theological, and other subjects. Hobbes had
been greatly pleased with Sorbières's translation : " The
book " (*i.e.*, the " De Cive "), he said, in his " Six
lessons to the professors of the mathematics," 1656,
" translated into French hath not only a great testimony
from the translator Sorbières, but also from Gassendus
and Mersennus." He began with Sorbières a correspondence in Latin, where he apostrophises him as
" clarissime charissimeque, amicissime, eruditissime,"
&c. And he went even further, as he dedicated " viro
clarissimo et amicissimo Samueli Sorberio," his " Dialogus

---

[1] In the biography he published as a preface to the " Sorberiana,"
Toulouse, 1691.

[2] " Les vrayes causes des derniers troubles d'Angleterre, abrégé
d'histoire, où les droicts du Roy et ceux du Parlement et du
peuple sont naïfvement représentez," Orange, 1653, 8vo. This is
often given as an original work of Sorbières, though in his dedication he himself states that he translated it at the request of the
Count de Dhona.

physicus de Natura Aeris," addressing to him a very characteristic and pungent letter, where, according to his wont, he loudly complains of everything and everybody, but concludes with the kindest appeal to his correspondent, saying : "Let us live as long and as well as we can, and let us love each other—Vale."

A desire of having some talk with Hobbes was among the main motives Sorbières had when he undertook the journey which was to make him for a short while famous all over Europe in the literary and diplomatic world, and to give him his "minute d'immortalité."

II.—SORBIÈRES'S JOURNEY.

Sorbières spent the summer of 1663 in England ; he had long conversations with Hobbes, he went to the play, dined at the French Embassy, was presented at Court, visited Oxford, drove to Hatfield, was admitted to a sitting of the Royal Society, and, when he had come back, wrote, at the request of the Marquis de Vaubrun Nogent, an account of all he had seen. The book appeared in 1664,[1] and raised a storm. The author was refuted, confuted, and exiled ; diplomatic

---

[1] "Relation d'un Voyage en Angleterre, où sont touchées plusieurs choses qui regardent l'estat des sciences, et de la Religion et autres matières curieuses." Paris, 1664, 8vo.

dispatches were exchanged on his account, and apology offered ; the English Court and the Danish Court and the French Court were in a state of commotion ; the literati on the three sides of the North Sea flew to their pens and made a stand against the invader ; even gentlemen belonging to the Church wrote in un-Christian language on the subject.

The book and man which created so much uproar have fallen since into oblivion. Whenever by any chance they are alluded to, it is always with a remembrance of the quarrel, and the " Relation d'un Voyage en Angleterre " is usually mentioned as being a book of slander on the English nation, and nothing more. But it *is* something more.

Sorbières's first impressions on landing had not been very good ; his companions' luggage had been stormed, it seems, by intrusive porters, and street arabs had pestered them with uncomplimentary apostrophs. The same thing, he philosophically observes, happens in all countries ; in England it happens thus : As soon as Frenchmen land, " boys run after them, shrieking, A mounser, a mounser ! *i.e.*, au monsieur ! by way of insult. Little by little, as travellers warm the boys through their very efforts to push them away or to stop their noise, the said boys rise to : French dogs, French dogs ! Such is the honourable name by which we are known in England—in the same way as we go by the name of *moucherons* [gnats] in Holland; both being less hard than the *matto Francese* [mad French] with which the rabble favours us in Italy."

For such inconveniences Sorbières considers that the travellers themselves are in a great measure responsible: " We make too much noise," he says ; " our agitation is considered indiscreet ; they deem it ridiculous and they show it as I have said. Our behaviour is the very reverse of theirs ; they are phlegmatic and quietly suffer everybody to do exactly as they like." This being once understood, no unpleasantness need be expected. Sorbières himself met with a better treatment at Dover than it had been his fortune to find anywhere else ; but his companions were greatly " déconcertés." For " as soon as they appeared on the wharf the noise they made with their servants drew a mob which accompanied them to their lodgings with strange howls. They took it unkindly ; dogs played their part in the fray ; stones were thrown, and the militia had to interfere."

From Dover to London, by way of Canterbury and Rochester, Sorbières is constantly on the look out, and writes, in praise of the English landscape, and especially on the beauty of the English grass, words which ought to have mollified the heart of his censors : " The country is undulated and shapes itself in hills and little valleys covered with an evergreen mantle. It even seemed to me that the grass had a more pleasant hue than elsewhere, and was finer. For this cause it is well fitted for the making of those pastures and sheets of grass so even that people play bowls on them as comfortably as they would on the cloth of some great billiard table. As this is the usual amusement of gentlemen in the country, they have large stone cylinders which they cause to be rolled on the grass to keep it down. All the country is full of parks, very pleasant to see, with large herds of deer pacing them. . . . There are so many trees that even the cultivated land has the appearance of a forest, when seen from some height, on account of the orchards and hedges with which the meadows and the fields are surrounded."

This will surely be considered an appreciative account ; though of course a British-born subject— such a subject, for example, as Thackeray—might have spoken more warmly, as the author of " Vanity Fair " did in his famous description of Dobbin's return from India, when the soldier passed " by pretty roadside inns, where the signs hung on the elms, and horses and waggoners were drinking under the chequered shadow of the trees ; by old halls and parks, rustic hamlets clustered round ancient grey churches, and through the charming friendly English landscape. Is there any in the world like it? To a traveller returning home it looks so kind—it seems to shake hands with you as you pass through it."

Sorbières and his companions go through villages and towns; they notice that the windows are low and without shutters, "which shows that the inhabitants do not fear insults nor revenge." The build of the windows is peculiar; at Canterbury, and indeed "all over England, they protrude and shape themselves into a sort of balcony, either polygonal or semi-circular; they appear as so many little towers and they give elegance to the outside of the houses when the eye has once become accustomed to them. The rooms are the more commodious for it and better lighted; and you can without being seen observe what goes on in the street. With us, people see only what is just opposite them."

Analogous to the differences in the national windows, Sorbières might have observed, were the difference between the literatures of the two countries: windows to see just opposite, with logical straightness, in Racine; polygonal or circular bay windows to see forward and backward, and all round, and to let the mind wander along with comers and goers ("that living flood pouring . . . from eternity onwards to eternity," says Teufelsdröck)—in Shake-speare. Not until the time of Victor Hugo and the romantic school was the use of bay-windows fairly re-established in French literature.

From Gravesend to London "dockyards are discovered on both sides of the road, and there is a swarm of carpenters who build ships. Ships of all sorts and of all ages are to be seen everywhere; their number is surprising."

III.—London Town.

Reaching town, Sorbières took lodgings in the Common Garden, and began his rambles in the capital, visiting it carefully and so to say street by street. Frenchmen, he considers, speak too disparagingly of it, the cause being that they do not know it well. The fact is (and he notes it with regret) that it is a larger one than Paris, but Paris possesses some other advantages, such as having a more numerous population. London has more houses and Paris more inhabitants, for in London there is only one family in each house. Furnished lodgings are, however, to be found, and they are not expensive, the cost being one crown (écu) per week. " I chose mine not far from Salisbury House because I liked to be able to visit at any time Mr. Hobbes, who was living there with his patron, the Earl of Devonshire, two very rare persons, of whom more hereafter."

London town is adorned with a number of grand buildings, such as the New Exchange in the "Strangh" (Strand). This is the place for mercers, "and I need not say whether fine wares are to be found there, as well as pretty girls at the counters." Lincoln's Inn Fields is pleasant to look at. Whitehall is a sorry medley of constructions of all epochs, but with a splendid banqueting-hall (Ingo Jones's banqueting-hall, with pictures by Rubens, now the Chapel Royal); the palace is beautifully situated near the river and the park. Two churches are to be noticed, one is Westminster Abbey with its chapel of Henry VII., handsomely carved (un ouvrage à roses) and its royal tombs, "which equal if they do not overmatch ours at St. Denis." The other church is "Pauls', for such is the unceremonious fashion in which this saint's church is called." The rest of the religious buildings consist of Protestant temples, very plain and without interest.

At Westminster, as well as on London Bridge, a remarkable sight is afforded by the heads of the late rebels stuck on the towers. "It is to be hoped that this sight will do as much to overawe evil-minded persons as the benedictions which have rained on the head of General Monk will encourage peace-loving, honourable and loyal citizens."

The parks are large and fine. In St. James's Park the king has caused telescopes to be erected, and Sorbières is allowed to use them and to contemplate Saturn with its ring and Jupiter with its moons. As for "Eyparc" (Hyde Park), it has too many "fiacres," and people who have their drive there turn round and round in endless gyrations, "de sorte que cela se passe avec peu de galanterie."

Little "galanterie" is to be discovered either in the cooking practices of the nation. "The English are not appreciative of cooking, and the table of the greatest lords is covered only with large pieces of meat. Bisques and potages are as good as unknown. . . . Pastry is heavy and ill-baked ; compotes and jams are scarcely eatable ; forks and ewers are not in common use ; the washing of the hands is performed by a dipping of them in a basin full of water that is brought round to all the guests. Towards the end of the meal it is customary to smoke tobacco (prendre du tabac en fumée), and while so doing people continue their talk very long. Men of quality do not practice smoking so assiduously as men of the people ; for a workman scarcely allows a day to pass without going to the tavern, there to smoke with some friends of his. For which reason, taverns abound and work progresses but slowly in the shops ; a tailor, a shoemaker will leave his board, whatever be the pressure of work, and stroll to the public-house, of evenings. And as he comes home late and somewhat dizzy, he opens his shutters and begins work again scarcely before seven the following morning. Manufactured goods are the dearer for it ; and a strange jealousy grows out of these towards French workmen, who are usually more diligent."

In their dining-rooms, as well as in their taverns, British citizens indulge in political talks of a very free description. They are proud of their Parliament, which is a " corps bigearre " ; and during the long hours they spend in smoking, they discuss public affairs, the new taxes, " the chimney tax," the state of the trade. Then they allow their fancy to carry them back to the time " when Oliver was there, and their fleets were so powerful, and they won glory on all the seas, and all the earth wanted their alliance, and the Republic flourished and received ambassadors from all countries." Then they consider the present state of the country and they make, between the past and the present, comparisons which are nothing short of " odieuses." They do not forbear saying what they think of the king himself; they are not unwilling to have one, but his rule must not press heavily upon them.

The theatres are well worth a visit; they are splendidly fitted up; the actors are excellent; the pity is that English dramatists have only contempt for the holy and mighty rule "of the twenty-four hours." Many characteristics of the play-house are peculiar to England. "The best places are in the pit, where men and women sit together, each with his friends. The theatre is very fine, and covered with green cloth; the stage is all left to the actors;[1] there are many perspectives and scene-shiftings. An orchestra plays and allows the audience to await, without *ennui*, the beginning of the performance; people go there early in order to hear the music. Actors and actresses are admirable, I am told, and so far as I could guess from their attitudes and pronunciation. But the plays would not meet with the same applause in France as they obtain in England. The poets despise uniformity of place and the rule of the twenty-four hours. They write comedies that are supposed to last twenty-five years; and when they have shown you the marriage of a

---

[1] The French stage had not been reformed yet in this respect: "Il y a à cette heure une incommodité épouvantable à la comédie; c'est que les deux côtés du théâtre sont tout pleins de jeunes gens assis sur des chaises de paille." Tallemant, "Historiette," cdxxxvi. *Cf.* Molière "J'étais sur le théâtre, en humeur d'écouter," &c.—"Les Facheux," 1 (1661).

prince at the first act, they exhibit all at once the fine deeds of his son, and they lead him far away to many lands. They pride themselves above all upon their good rendering of the various passions, vices and virtues, and in this they succeed rather well. . . . Their comedies are in *prose mesurée* [*i.e.*, blank verse], which is nearer the ordinary language than our verses. They cannot conceive that it is not a teasing trouble to have the same cadence constantly striking on one's ear. They pretend that to bear for two or three hours Alexandrine verses, with the regular cæsura stop, cannot be considered either very natural or pleasant. It must be confessed that this way of speech is as far from real life and by consequence from what is to be represented, as the Italian custom of acting comedies in music [*i.e.*, operas] outdoes the extravagance of our own habits. But it is better not to discuss tastes, and we must leave everybody to follow his own bend."

So great, indeed, is the difference between English and French plays, that Sorbières would bring home some samples of the former to show to his friends at Paris as travelling curiosities. What he chose to take with him was neither the first folio of Shakespeare nor old Ben's works, nor Davenant's romantic plays, but of all works and of all dramatists, a volume lately published by "dear Margaret Newcastle," as Charles Lamb was fond of calling her; " un volume que la Marquise de Nieucastel a composé." He took at the same time with him three volumes of the poetical, political, and philosophical works " de cette dame," and his friends in France could not but admire the " bel esprit, good sense, and eloquence," of which he says they are full.

Other sights attract crowds in London ; foremost among them the fights, of what Sorbières calls " gladiateurs " ; but we shall pass them over, for, as he says, they have " quelque chose de bien farouche," [1] and we must go back and mix with polite society and learned men.

London town is not famous only for its buildings,

[1] " Je ne dois pas oublier, parmi les divertissement de la bonne ville de Londres ceux que l'on va prendre . de temps en temps à voir les gladiateurs. Ce sont d'ordinaire des maistres d'escrime ou des prévosts de sale qui, pour se mettre en réputation et gaigner autre chose que des coups font un défi et proposent 20 ou 30 Jacobus à qui vondra se battre contre eux. L'argent est mis en dépôt et remis à celuy qui accepte le combat. L'appellant tire ce qui est receu à la porte du cirque, et quelque fois il monte à deux ou trois fois plus qu'il n'a donné à son antagoniste, selon qu'il y a plus ou moins de peuple qui accourt à ce spectacle. Ils combattent avec la rondache et l'espée, à grand coups d'estramaçon : mais je croy qu'il y a de la collusion entre eux pour faire durer le jeu que l'on quitte volontiers au premier sang répandu. D'ailleurs le fer n'est pas esmoulu, et néantmoins ils ne laissent pas de se donner quelque fois de terribles horions et de s'avaler la moitié d'une joue . . . En ce triste diverstissement, il y [a] quelque chose de bien farouche."

but also for its *men;* it is pre-eminently " magna virum." Towering above all the rest in the estimation of Sorbières, and of many, the great Mr. Hobbes, of Malmesbury, was then to be seen. " The first thing I did when I reached London was to go and visit Mr. Hobbes. . . . I had not seen him for fourteen years; I found him little altered. He was sitting in his room in the same posture as he was accustomed to, of afternoons, when he lived in Paris ; for he spent that time of the day in studying, after he had been walking all the morning. He acted thus for the benefit of his health, which he rightly deemed the first thing to be considered. For the same cause, and though he is now seventy-eight, he has modified his rules in only one item, adding each week a game at tennis, which he continues until he has to stop out of sheer exhaustion. He is little changed in his face, and not at all in what concerns the vigour of his mind, the strength of his memory, and the mirthfulness of his temper, which he has preserved in their entirety." [1]

---

[1] " Je trouvay le premier [*i.e.,* Hobbes] peu changé depuis quatorze ans que je ne l'avois veu, et je le rencontray dans sa chambre en la même posture qu'il était accoutumé d'estre toutes les après disnées ; car il les employoit à l'estude, après s'estre promené tout le matin. Ce qu'il practiquoit pour sa santé, laquelle il faisoit avec raison marcher la première ; comme encore à présent dans sa soixante et dix huictiesme année il n'a adjousté

The king favours him greatly. "His Majesty showed me his portrait by the hand of Cooper [1] in his cabinet of natural and mechanical curiosities. He asked me whether I knew that person and what I thought of him. I answered as I should, and we agreed that if he had been a little less dogmatical he would have been very useful as a member of the Royal Society. . . . He has frightened, I do not know how, the clergy of his country and the mathematicians of Oxford and their followers. For which reason his Majesty told me that he looked very much like a bear baited by dogs."

Many other philosophers, thinkers, and inventors are to be met in London; and, indeed, "in all times England has produced excellent minds who have addicted themselves to an earnest study of natural sciences. Had the country produced in this line but Gilbert, Harvey, and Bacon, it would be enough for her to compete with France and Italy, who had Galileo, Descartes and Gassendi. But to speak truth Bacon the

à ceste méthode que l'exercice de la paulme à laquelle il joue une fois toutes les semaines jusques à ce qu'il succombe à la lassitude. Il me parut fort peu changé de visage, et point du tout quant à la vigueur de l'esprit, à la mémoire et à la gayeté qu'il retenoit toute entière."

[1] Samuel Cooper, the well-known miniaturist, 1609–72, who painted portraits of Cromwell, Charles II., &c.

Chancellor rose above all the others by the vastness of his ideas." No one did so much for physical science and so powerfully incited people to make experiments. Private persons, however, do nothing but ruin themselves in such attempts, and before success could be reached it was necessary to wait until princes and lords had acquired a taste for things of this sort. The Commonwealth, Sorbières observes, came in good time to give leisure to princes; they began studying sciences; "even the king did not neglect them, and he has acquired a knowledge at which I was surprised when I was received by his Majesty." The proof Sorbières gives of Charles' scientific tastes show, however, as might have been surmised, that the monarch was fond of curiosities and *lusus naturæ*, but did not trouble himself very much about the solution of higher problems.

Of a more serious nature were Sorbières's conversations with another friend of his, M. de Montconis, the well-known traveller and savant, who made him *au fait* with all the more recent discoveries. Sorbières is thus shown an instrument which marks "the changes in the atmosphere" and registers them with a pencil; he receives an account of a deaf and dumb person whom M. Wallis of Oxford had taught to read. He is let into the secret of a new plan to "pétarder," *i.e.*,

blow up, ships at sea.   He sees a machine newly in-
invented by the Marquess of Worcester, " which being
set in motion by one single man, will raise at a height
of forty feet, in one minute, four great buckets full of
water."   He becomes acquainted with members of the
Royal Society ; he is admitted to one of their sittings,
and he is filled with admiration by their learning as
well as by their modesty.   " These excellent men are
full of high thoughts, and they put in practice with
great cleverness what they have conceived in their
mind."

The Royal Society, or, as Sorbières calls it, the
" Académie Royale," was then in its early youth,
having received its charter only the year before.   It
held its sittings in Gresham College every Wednesday,
in a street which our traveller is pleased to call " la rue
Biscop getstriidt " (Bishopsgate Street).   " The hall
of assembly is a large one, all wainscoted.   There is a
long table before the chimney, with seven or eight
chairs covered with grey cloth, and two rows of wood
benches, all bare, with a *dossier ;* they are arranged so
as to rise amphitheatre-wise. . . . The president sits
in the middle of the table in an armchair, with his back
to the chimney ; the secretary sits at one end, on the
left ; they have an inkstand and some paper before
them.   I saw nobody on the chairs.   I suppose they

are reserved for men of high rank or for those who have to come and speak to the president on certain occasions. All the other academicians sit anywhere without ceremony ; and when one of them comes in after the sitting has begun, no one moves, the president nods to him, and he sits down quietly on the first seat, in order not to interrupt the speaker. The president has a little wooden mace in his hand with which he knocks on the table when he wants silence. . . . Speakers are never interrupted, and those who disagree do not carry the discussion to a point nor use a tone that might be considered disobliging. Nothing more civil, more decent, and better conducted than this assembly as I saw it can well be conceived."

Of all this Sorbières judged as best he could, by the tone of the speeches and the manner of the speakers, and by hints which friends gave him as to the purport of the discussion. For we need not say that he did not understand a word of English ; nobody did in his time; his main resource when his learned acquaintances did not speak French was Latin, but even this did not prove very satisfactory, for " the English pronounce Latin with a peculiar accent which renders it no less difficult to understand than their own language."

IV.—Out of Town.

Before leaving England Sorbières resolved to see two very characteristic sights, namely, one of the universities and one " château." He took accordingly a " carrosse" and drove to Oxford. The drive was performed in two days. " We were warned against highwaymen ; I thought at first that they mentioned them out of sheer pride, to show that London was nothing behind Paris in this respect. But I heard that there was some truth in the statement, and that highwaymen make their appearance from time to time." They live, however, under difficulties, and country people chase and destroy them mercilessly.

At Oxford, Sorbières is shown all over the place by the obliging Mr. Lockey, a "sharp and learned professor," who lives at Christ College, and is "Bibliothécaire d'Oxfordt." [1] He visits with the help of this guide college after college, "the meanest of which is scarcely inferior to the Sorbonne." He greatly admires the Bodleian Library, St. John's College, and Brasenose. "There is one college where I saw a big bronze nose above the door, similar to a mask of

---

[1] Thomas Lockey, D.D., librarian of the Bodleian Library, 1660–65. He had, according to Sorbières, "pris à la cour de France un air obligeant et une façon accorte."

Polichinelle. I was told that the place was called on this account the college of the nose, and that within its walls John Duns Scot had lectured in his time : to commemorate which event a reproduction of his nose had been stuck above the door."

In his rambles about Oxford Sorbières meets Dr. Wallis, who, being the adversary of Hobbes, is very severely handled by the traveller. Wallis is confessed to be very learned indeed, but his manners are rough and uncivil ; he has " bien moins que M. Hobbes du galant homme." He wears on his head a not unknown sort of coiffure, by which, however, M. Sorbières seems to have been deeply struck. " You should see him," he says, " with his flat cap on his head, as if he had covered his portfolio with black cloth and sewed it to his *calotte.* Such a sight would have inclined you to laughter, as much as the appearance and courtesy of my friend Mr. Hobbes would have bred in you esteem and affection for him."

The " château " which Sorbières visited is called by him Achtfields (Hatfield). He is taken there by the Earl of Devonshire, the pupil of Hobbes; the distance from London is eighteen miles ; they go and dine there and come back in the same day, performing the journey " à toute bride."

Hatfield is a delightful place. " The eye meets on

all sides woods, meadows, and hills and vales. . . . I
rarely ever saw a more agreeable solitude. The castle
is built in bricks with several turrets covered with lead
and slates. There are three base courts, in the first
of which are the stables and the ménagerie. When
you reach the place from the main avenue on the park
side, and when all the gates of the courts are open, you
discover beyond the architectural foreground endless
alleys cut straight to the other extremity of the park.
The castle looks prodigiously gay and the inside is
magnificent. I numbered fifteen rooms on the same
floor very well furnished, also a gallery and a chapel.
We dined in a hall which overlooks a grass parterre
with two fountains and espaliers on the sides, and a
balustrade opposite with flower pots and statues on it.
From this parterre you are led down to another by two
flights of twelve or fifteen steps each, and then to
a third."

There is a large "parterre d'eau," then a meadow
with troops of deer, and then hills covered with a
wood which closes the horizon. There are a variety
of kiosks and bowers, so pretty, so fine, overlooking
such a clear and pure course of water that, suddenly
growing lyrical, Sorbières goes on to describe "the
little fishes who come in their thousands to enjoy so
many delights ; they try to leave their own element,

and they jump out of the water as if wanting to contemplate all I have just described." [1]

Hatfield, in a word, is an " enchanted place."

V.—Sorbières's " Impression d'ensemble."

Taken altogether, Sorbières's conclusions are rather fair and modest.   If we except some unlucky *boutades*, his general impression is greatly in favour of the nation he had been visiting.   He honestly acknowledges that many things are against him for giving a reliable judgment.   He has seen, it is true, the king and the court ; he has moved about as much as he could, paid visits in the country, spoken with people of all sorts, and kept his eyes well open.   But his stay has been too short ; his ignorance of the language has been very much against him, so that some of his strictures are, he confesses, only from hearsay.   " Though I took all the possible trouble, I do not persuade myself that I have gone to the bottom of affairs, nor understood a nation whose temper is very singular and uneven.   I report things as they *appeared* to me ; not, may be, as they are in the *vérité des choses*."

In his summary of the defects and qualities of the

---

[1] See French text in Appendix III.

nation the part allotted to praise is no small one.
Among the former he notices a tendency to idleness,
presumption, and " quelque sorte d'extravagance de
pensée qui se remarque même dans leurs plus excel-
lents écrits." But he is careful to add that the nation
should not be blamed for those faults ; they all come,
he says, anticipating Taine's theories, " from the soil"
(*terroir*).[1] Do not forget besides that " il y a en eux
de très rares qualités." " I find in them a something
that is great, and reminds one of ancient Rome. . . .
They have a deep love for their country ; they are
strongly united against foreigners ; they are intrepid in
danger." They are ruled by a king now, but " ils ont
beaucoup retenu, en se rangeant sous l'estat de l'em-
pire, de l'humeur qui domine naturellement dans les
esprits de tous les hommes en l'estat de liberté."
They have, indeed, a propensity to scorn all the rest
of the world ; this blameable tendency is mainly caused
by the extraordinary resources afforded by their own
country, which " lacks neither iron, nor stone, lead,
tin, coal, plaster, wood, corn, vegetables, meadows,
oxen, sheep, horses, game, pasture-land, springs and
rivers, nor plenty of fine sights, nor industry to turn
all these into use, . . . with the ocean round them to

[1] "Cette inclination de laquelle je ne prétends pas les blâmer
puisque elle leur vient du terroir. . . ."

prevent other nations from coming to trouble their felicity."

Thinking thus of the nation at large, and considering that some *boutades* here and there would be counted as nothing, Sorbières, when he had come back to his country, did not hesitate to write and publish an account of what he had seen, with results which were not long in following and which surprised him not a little.

VI.—Sorbières publishes his Book. The Consequences of the Deed.

Sorbières's book was printed at Paris in 1664 ; the dedication to the king is dated December 12, 1663 : the "*achevé d'imprimer*" is of May 16, 1664. A storm, extraordinary in its violence, was at once raised by the work.

The jealousy between France and England was then keener than ever ; there was, as the phrase is, no love lost between the two countries, which phrase plain Mr. Pepys plainly wrote in different words, thus : "We do naturally hate the French." Of that hate the Sun-King, for reasons of his own, would have none. The thing he wanted then above all others, the plan nearest and dearest to his heart, was a close alliance and union with the British Kingdom. A number of sacrifices which under different circumstances he would have never dreamed of making counted for nothing, if only he could reach his most cherished goal. In such a cause to give up some Sorbières or other was for him no sacrifice, and his decision would depend not on what was in the book, but on what would be thought of it in England.

Unluckily for Sorbières his performance was very badly received in London. In the jealous mood of the nation the merest pretext was seized upon for recrimination. All Sorbières had said of the Roman temper of the English and of their manifold virtues and glories was as nothing ; his *boutades* and some slanderous remarks, not even always his own, but mostly reported, were alone regarded. The outcry was especially loud because of his language concerning the Chancellor. What he had said was nothing more nor less than this : " My Lord Hidde is a man of the law, an advocate by profession ; he understands the legal procedure well, but he knows little of other things ; he is ignorant of the *belles lettres.* He is said to be presbyterian in his character, and to want distinction in his mind (*il a l'esprit populaire*). He is a good-looking man, with an agreeable presence ; he is about sixty ; he has the honour to be father-in-law to the Duke of York, which is, maybe, one of his crimes in the eyes of the Earl of Bristol and of the people."

This picture of the Prime Minister was declared to constitute in itself an unbearable and unpardonable offence. King and Court and Chancellor rose against Sorbières. To add to the author's misfortunes he had towards the end of his volume introduced a story of the Danish king and the Count Ulefeld, which made him obnoxious to the Danish as well as to the English Court.

His fate was soon settled. On the 9th of July, 1664, the king being at Fontainebleau, an edict of the Council of State was issued "against a book entitled ' Relation [etc.],' written by the Sieur de Sorbières, to the disadvantage of the English nation and of the King of Denmark."

The edict itself condemns in no measured terms a work " in which the author, under pretence of recounting with complete simplicity what he has seen, takes the liberty to put forth a variety of things which are contrary to truth and detrimental to the English nation. He is so bold as to express himself calumniously concerning the personal qualities and the behaviour of one of the principal ministers of the King of Great Britain, the said minister being deeply esteemed, considered, and beloved by his Majesty. . . ." The author is also guilty of some inconsiderate judgments bearing upon the conduct of the King of Denmark ; and for all these reasons "his said Majesty in his council, with the intent of showing publicly the displeasure he felt for this audacious and imprudent satire—the author of which has already been sentenced to relegation—has ordered and orders the said book . . . to be suppressed in all his kingdom and lands belonging to him, forbids all printers and booksellers to sell and publish the same under a penalty of five hundred livres, wills that all his subjects of whatsoever rank bring the copies they may possess to the office of their respective baillages and sénéchaussées, to be, as above said, suppressed. . . . Signed : Louis, and lower, De Lionne, and sealed with the great seal of yellow wax *sur simple queue.*"

Very mournfully did Sorbières undertake his journey to Brittany, vainly protesting of his innocence and good intentions. He stopped at Nantes, and from thence wrote the most pressing letters to his friends in Paris to exculpate himself and to ask for their interference in his favour. Some are still extant (and unpublished) ; one directed to the famous Abbé de Pure, the *bête noire* of Boileau, is preserved in the original at the National Library, Paris. In it Sorbières throws himself on his knees, beseeching the abbé to protect him and to set his numerous patrons in motion to procure the repeal of the decree ; the said patrons being " les plus honnêtes gens de la cour, du palais et des académies." A special appeal to "les marquises" is not forgotten (Nantes, August 9, 1664).[1]

While Sorbières was thus eating the bread of adversity, his book, though suppressed, continued to live, and as it was prohibited in France, foreign booksellers were not slow to seize their opportunity. A variety of editions were published, in French, in Italian, in English. Replies and imitations increased its repute, and, in most cases, increased also the ill-humour on both sides. Some of the replies were in French, such as the " Observations d'un Gentilhomme Anglois sur le voyage d'Angleterre du Sieur Sorbière," [2] which has all the appearance of a work *de commande.* The author is

---

[1] MS. Français, 15209, fol. 13. Another among the famous adversaries of Boileau busied himself with Sorbières, but was less favourably inclined. Chapelain writes to Heinsius, then at Stockholm : " Le Sieur Sorbière est toujours relégué à Nantes où il ronge son frein et paye la peine de son insolence. M. Huygens le père qui revient d'Angleterre m'a dit que le chancelier se relaschoit et vouloit bien lui pardonner sa témérité. Je ne croy pas que le roy de Danemark soit si facile," October 20, 1664. " Lettres," ed. Tamizey de Larroque, Paris, 1883, 2 vols. 4to, vol. ii. p. 371.

[2] Paris, 1664, 12mo. See also : " Réponse aux faussetés et invectives qui se lisent dans la Relation du voyage de Sorbières en Angleterre." Amsterdam, 1675, 12mo. It is an adaptation of Sprat's " Observations." Also " A Journey to London in the year 1698 . . . written . . . by Monsieur Sorbières, and newly translated." London, 1698, 8vo. The real author of this last work was William King ; Sorbières at that date had been dead for twenty-eight years.

loud in his praise of "the Solomon of our century, the august King Louis XIV.," and of Lionne, a minister without peer. The drift of the answer is that if Sorbières has discovered vices (as well as qualities) in the English nation, his opinion is an isolated one, and a number of authors are quoted to show that the French have never discovered anything but virtue in their neighbours.

There were English answers, too, and these were couched in less measured language. For a while, owing to the interference of the French Ambassador, the Comte de Cominges, no replies were allowed to be printed, and Charles ordered the materials collected with this object to be brought to him and set aside. But at length the monarch's will was altered or overruled, and Thomas Sprat printed his " Observations on Monsieur de Sorbières's voyage into England—Sed poterat tutior esse domi" (1665, another edition 1668). It is a wild, rambling pamphlet, written *ab irato*, the lapse of time having in no way cooled the anger of the author. Sprat is blinded by his passion ; his answers in several cases defeat his own intentions, so much so that more actual praise of the English nation will be found in Sorbières's book than in Sprat's wild reply.

Sprat acknowledges the fairness of Louis XIV. ; his treatment of Sorbières " became the justice of so great a monarch," and befitted the sins of the traveller. These sins are manifold ; he is a man of an obscure birth, a turncoat (Sprat was forgetting his own " Poem on the death of Oliver, late Lord Protector," 1659), a pedant, and an ass ; his descriptions of the country are grotesque ; the account (quoted above) he gives of Kent is worthy of " the authors of Clelia or Astrea." His pretence that the king and court have a propensity to spend too much money, and that this causes discontent in the country, is monstrous ; for everybody knows that Charles has greatly reduced the expenses of the Crown, and dismissed all useless persons that were wont to hang about court : " those blood suckers have parted with their very food." Sorbières's attack on Clarendon is a scandal ; he pretends that the chancellor is merely a " man of the law"; this surely is bad enough, " but the worst is still behind : *my Lord Chancellor is utterly ignorant of the Belles Lettres!* " Four pages are dedicated to a vindication of Clarendon's character in this respect. The description of Dr. Wallis's cap is considered a gross insult to the University and the nation at large. So blinded, indeed, had Sprat been by anger, that he makes the most curious mistakes in reading the French text of his opponent. When Sorbières complains that the Dutch irreverently call the French " moucherons," Sprat declares that the French are nicknamed " mushrooms."

What Sorbières advanced concerning the English stage touched Sprat to the quick ; the English not to know and properly revere the unities ! This showed the man Sorbières was ! And not caring in the least what great men he was throwing overboard, and how detrimental if true his own strictures would have been to England, Sprat thus vindicates the drama of his country. That Frenchman, he says, " has confounded the reign of Charles II. with that of Queen Elizabeth. 'Tis true about an hundred years ago the English poets were not very exact in such decencies ; but no more than were the dramatists of any other countries. The English themselves did laugh away such absurdities as soon as any, and for these last fifty years our stage has been as regular in those circumstances as the best of Europe. Seeing he thinks fit to upbraid our present poets with the errors of which their predecessors were guilty so long since, I might as justly impute the vile absurdities that are to be found in Amadis de Gaul, to Monsieur de Corneille, de Scudéry, de Chapelain, de Voiture, and the rest of the famous moderne French wits."

Having thus dealt equal if summary justice to Amadis and to Shakespeare, Sprat goes on to remind his friend, Dr. Wren, that, discussing together, some day, long before, what time they would have preferred to live in, they had agreed the time of Augustus would have been the best. " This, sir, was then our opinion ; but it was before the King's return. For since that blessed time the condition of our own country appears to me to be such that we need not search into ancient history for a real idea of happinesse." Sprat was appointed Canon of Windsor in 1680, Dean of Westminster in 1683, and Bishop of Rochester in 1684 :— the least, in truth, which could be done.

Long before this, however, Charles, who had not the defect of a sour temper, considered the poor Sorbières had paid enough for his insufficient appreciation of Clarendon's Belles Lettres. He requested the French Ambassador to interfere in favour of the culprit, who was accordingly amnestied.

Sorbières came back to Paris, went to Rome in 1667, where a portrait of him was made by the famous Audran, and continued as vainly as before his exertions to establish his fortune. Having become dropsical with no hope of recovery (1670) he took laudanum in order to " stun himself," and not to suffer the pangs of agony ; and thus he died—" too much as a philosopher," says Moreri.

CLEMENCY OF HENRY IV. AT THE BATTLE OF IVRY, FROM THE
LONDON EDITION OF THE "HENIADE."

V.

ONE MORE DOCUMENT CONCERNING VOLTAIRE'S VISIT TO ENGLAND.

WHEN Voltaire, after his second imprisonment in the Bastille, had to leave his country and go to England [1] (1726), he found there his friend, Lord Bolingbroke. He had known the late minister of Queen Anne in France, when that statesman and philosopher lived in exile, and he was heartily welcomed by him. Bolingbroke, who was "amy zélé, dangereux ennemy," [2] lost no time in introducing

---

[1] On Voltaire's visit to England, see J. Churton Collins, "Bolingbroke, a historical study, and Voltaire in England," London, 1886; and A. Ballantyne, "Voltaire's visit to England 1726-9," London, 1893.

[2] Portrait of Bolingbroke in an unpublished note by the Duke d'Aumont, French Ambassador to England, August 10, 1712. Archives of the French Foreign Office, "Angleterre," vol. ccxcii. : "A parler juste, on peut dire que c'est mylord Bolingbroke qui, après le Grand Trésorier (*i.e.*, Harley) a le plus de crédit et qui gouverne tout. Il est amy intime du Grand Trésorier, il a des talents supérieurs. Il est homme polye, éloquent et s'estoit acquis par ces

Voltaire, an exile in his turn, into the most elegant society. He introduced him also, and this was no less useful to the new-comer, into the literary circles of London. Voltaire thus became acquainted with Swift, Pope, Gay, and many others.

One fact has never been noticed. Voltaire, who rightly enough asserted, on leaving France, that he was "very well recommended to people in England," [1] had provided himself, before he crossed the Channel, with letters of introduction for the French Ambassador. They had been given him by none other than the Foreign Minister himself, Count de Morville, a member of the French Academy, the same to whom he announced a little later the impending, but never-to-take-place, visit of Dean Swift to France. M. de Morville had even gone the length of asking the royal ambassador to present Voltaire to the members of the English cabinet, so that the exile was soon on the best of terms with everybody : with the Tories, thanks to Bolingbroke, and with the Whigs, owing to the good offices of M. de Morville. Walpole, among others, patroned him with great zeal.

raisons un crédit extraordinaire dans la chambre basse pendant qu'il y tenoit scéance. D'ailleurs il aime les plaisirs, son commerce est agréable, il dit son sentiment avec beaucoup de hardiesse et de liberté. Il est amy zélé, dangereux ennemy."

[1] To Thiériot, August 12, 1726.

Letters of this sort recommending a banished man to the kindness and good offices of his ambassador would shock our ideas ; but such an occurrence did not seem so very strange then, and this example is not unique. There was no more shame at that time in being exiled than in being " embastillé," and it was not very rare to see friendly, not to say cordial, relations established between proscribed Frenchmen and the representatives of the most Christian monarch. Expelled from France on account of some writing, for which he had to undergo a life-long exile, Saint-Évremond had been cordially received by the French Ambassador, who never failed to send news of him, his doings, his sayings, and his health, to Louis XIV., adding even the most favourable appreciation of the author of the " Lettre au Marquis de Créquy." The Chevalier de Grammont was equally well treated at the French Embassy, and Count Cominges was good enough to give him kindly advice, and strongly to recommend him not to marry the peerless but portion-less Mademoiselle de Hamilton.

Voltaire seems to have availed himself of Morville's letters in at least one memorable circumstance. The ambassador was the Comte, afterwards Marshal and Duke, de Broglie. The occasion was the issuing of a definitive edition of the " Henriade." This epic had already been issued five times on the Continent; but these editions, three of which bore the imprint of Geneva, and two of Amsterdam (1723–4), did not contain a perfectly complete text. Voltaire had revised his work, and had been preparing for several years to give an enlarged version, which he intended to publish "in quarto, on beautiful paper, with large margins, and handsome type." [1]

The moment seemed auspicious; the ground had been prepared by Voltaire himself, who, in order to be better known among English thinkers and wits, had just printed two essays in English: "An essay upon the civil wars of France, extracted from curious manuscripts, and also upon the epick poetry of the European nations from Homer down to Milton," by M. de Voltaire, London, 1727. The new epic poet had a pecuniary as well as a literary interest to make the best of the occasion. A fashion, which had been introduced also into France, [2] had prevailed for some thirty years in England. Literary works of importance were published by subscription; it was a more decent means of getting money from admirers and friends than the dedications of old. Famous authors were thus enabled to collect

[1] To Thiériot, October 17, 1725.

[2] "Tout le monde sait," Abbé Prévost writes, "que c'est à Londres que la méthode des souscriptions a pris naissance." "Le Pour et Contre," No. vi.

sums which, given the difference in the value of money, can be compared with the profits of the most popular novelists of our day. The time was long past when that poor author, Milton, had published his " Paradise Lost," with great and immediate success, and a total profit of eighteen pounds for him and his widow. Dryden, since then, had printed by subscription his translation of Virgil in 1697, and had received twelve hundred pounds ; Pope had got nearly nine thousand for his Homer ; Prior four thousand for a volume of poems ; Gay was going to secure one thousand for a single comedy, " Polly," the performance of which, it is true, had been forbidden by authority.

Voltaire was in a state of very pressing need. His pensions had been stopped, and, on his coming to London, the failure of the Jew, d'Acosta, had cost him twenty thousand francs. He at once resolved to turn to account this taste of a wealthy public for literary things, and to realise an idea he already entertained before his exile.[1] He advertised a fine quarto edition of the " Henriade," with engravings, and began to enlist subscribers, at a guinea each. A curious letter, addressed by him to Swift at that moment, which figures in his " Correspondance Générale," shows that he did not forget to knock at the door of his literary

[1] To Thiériot, 1722.

friends. He asks Swift " to make use of the influence he enjoys in Ireland to secure some subscribers to the ' Henriade,' now entirely finished, which, for the lack of some slight assistance, has not yet been published." December 14, 1727.

He sent also his appeal to his political friends. Walpole took the interests of the poet greatly to heart ; Bolingbroke did the same, and displayed the more zeal because he had been " infiniment satisfait " with the epic, when Voltaire had shown him a first sketch of it at the castle of La Source in Touraine, 1722.

Voltaire, lastly, had called upon the representative of his country and asked him to secure subscribers for the work. The ambassador who, before he had come to London in a diplomatic capacity, had busied himself much more with war than with poetry, was greatly puzzled, for he did not know whether the epic of that " Sieur de Voltaire " was worthy of approval. He therefore referred the matter to his chief, the French Foreign Minister, and asked for instructions. His letter to the Comte de Morville is preserved in the archives of the Ministère des Affaires Étrangères, Paris, and has escaped the notice of all the biographers of Voltaire. It is to the following effect :—

"From London, March 3, 1727.

"Sir,—The Sieur de Voltaire whom you did me the honour to recommend to me, and in favour of whom you sent me letters of recommendation introducing him to the ministers of this Court, is about to print in London, by subscription, his poem on the League. He asks me to secure subscribers for him, and M. de Walpole does his very best on his part to get him as many as possible. I should greatly like to please him ; but I have not seen that work, and I do not know whether the Court will approve of the additions and suppressions he has introduced into the text given to the public at Paris, and of the plates he has ordered to be sent from thence in order to adorn the same. I told him therefore that I could not meddle with his undertaking, till I knew whether you liked it or not. I am always afraid that French authors should be tempted to make a wrongful use of the liberty they enjoy in a country like this, to write all that comes into their mind concerning religion, the Pope, the Government or the members of it. Poets especially are wont to use such license without caring much whether or no they cast obloquy upon what is most sacred. And if there were anything of that sort in this poem I should not like to incur the blame of having subscribed to it and recommended others to do the same. I most humbly beseech you, sir, to be so good as to send me instructions concerning the line I must follow in this circumstance. I shall conform my conduct to what you will do me the honour to prescribe.

" I have, &c ,

" BROGLIE."[1]

This great circumspection on the part of the soldier and diplomatist was only too well justified. In no other period had the produce of the printing press been watched in France with a more searching eye. Voltaire knew it well, as he had already tried in vain to obtain a royal privilege for that same " Henriade," and had had to cause the copies of it to be secretly carried from Rouen to Paris, where they were to be sold. " The narrowness of mind of our authorities," he wrote later, " has reached such a pitch that only meaningless works can be freely printed. The good authors of the time of Louis the Fourteenth would be denied the ' privilege.' Boileau and La Bruyère would receive nothing but persecutions. We must live for ourselves and for our friends, be careful not to think aloud, or, if we want to do so, go and think in England or Holland "[2]— the very thing Count de Broglie feared Voltaire was

---

[1] See Appendix iv.
[2] To M. de Formont, 1734

about to do. The epic on Henry the Fourth had
been, as M. Desnoiresterres has pointed out, considered as imbued with a " Jansenist," nay, a " semi-
Pelagian " spirit. The praise it contained of heretical
Elizabeth, and of the Huguenot chief, Coligny, had
also caused deep disgust to pious-minded persons.

As for the engravings, if there was nothing to say
concerning those which represented the clemency of the
king at Ivry (reproduced in my volume), or " King
Henry the Fourth, lifelike, on a throne of clouds, with
King Louis the Fifteenth in his arms,"[1] several others
lent themselves to criticism. The author had ordered,
for example, the goddess Discord to be shown in one
of them as newly arrived from Rome, and inciting the
monks of Paris to armed rebellion.

I have vainly looked for the answer of M. de
Morville. Comte de Broglie in fact abstained from
subscribing to the book, and his name does not appear
in the list published with it. The poem was issued in
1728, under the title : " La Henriade de M. de
Voltaire "—" à Londres." Some copies had been
subscribed for by French gentlemen ; they were sent
to them from London, but on reaching the opposite
shore they were seized and confiscated by the royal
authorities.

[1] Voltaire to Thiériot, September 11, 1722.

The success of the undertaking was, however, very great in England. In the table of subscribers may be found, besides the names of many colleagues of the Comte de Broglie — that is to say, members of the Corps Diplomatique—innumerable names of honourable and right honourable gentlemen, lords, earls, dukes, and duchesses, obviously enlisted by Bolingbroke, Walpole, and the other powerful friends of Voltaire. Chesterfield subscribed for ten copies and Bolingbroke for twenty.

Many men of letters find a place also in this brilliant pageant of names, and among others, Swift, Tickell, Cibber, Berkeley, Lady Mary Wortley Montagu, John Locke, Congreve, &c. Swift seems to have exerted himself with great alacrity in favour of the writer, who bestowed upon him the praise of being " Rabelais dans son bon sens." The large number of people with a situation in Ireland appearing in the list is a proof of the Dean's friendly activity. " I do not send you yet my great edition," we read in one of Voltaire's English letters, " because I am really afraid of having not copies enough to answer the calls of the subscribers."

More than that : King George the Second and Queen Caroline, "the virtuous consort," as Voltaire wrote in his dedication of the " Henriade," " of one who, among so many crowned heads, enjoys, almost

alone, the inestimable honour of ruling a free nation,"
bestowed their patronage on the work of the exile.
Besides the large paper issue, it went through three
editions in three weeks, and the sums Voltaire thus
received were the beginning of his fortune, that is to
say, of his independence.

APPENDIX.

APPENDIX

APPENDIX.

I.

MEDIÆVAL SHIPPING.

(See above, pp. 43 ff.)

M. CH. DE LA RONCIÈRE, of the Paris National Library, one of the best authorities on mediæval shipping, whom I had consulted about the "navy" sent to Scotland to fetch the Dauphiness, kindly wrote in reply the following letter, which will surely be read with interest :—

" . . . Il était naturel de se demander pourquoi le roi d'Écosse prisait tant les galères et si les galères espagnoles n'étaient pas supérieures aux autres.

" Remarquons d'abord qu'en 1435 il n'y avait plus de galères de guerre ni en France ni en Angleterre. Depuis Richard II., les rois anglais n'en avaient plus. La liste des vaisseaux d'Henri IV. et Henri V. ne comprend que des voiliers (carraques, nefs, balingères) vendus du reste en 1423.

" En France, la marine royale avait toujours compté de 6 à 15 galères pendant plus d'un siècle. Mais les deux derniers spécimens de ce type avaient été brûlés en 1418 avec le Clos des Galées lui même, lors de la prise de Rouen.

" Du reste, cette année même où le roi d'Écosse songeait aux galères espagnoles, un autre souverain y pensait aussi. Je veux dire le duc de Bourgogne Philippe le Bon qui, dès 1436 aura cinq ou six galères achetées dans le Sud ou construites par des méridionaux.

"Les États du nord-ouest de l'Europe, en 1435, ne possédaient donc pas de galères. Ils n'avaient—et le roi d'Écosse tout le premier—ils n'avaient dis-je, comme bâtiments à rames, que des *row-barges*, filles des *longues nefs* norroises. Mais les row-barges avaient leurs bordages à elins et non pas à joints lisses, comme les sveltes galères du Sud ; elles étaient plus fortes, mais plus lourdes ; elles avaient beaucoup moins de rameurs que les galères, quatre vingts au plus, tandis que les galères en avaient jusqu'à deux cents. Les row-barges enfin n'avaient pas reçu ces perfectionnements et cet agrandissement qui, au XVe siècle, leur vaudront, d'être placées au rang des plus rapides croiseurs. Ce que les historiens disent de ces row-barges ou ramberges anglaises qui combattirent d'Annebault en 1545 n'est pas applicable aux petites row-barges de 1435.

"Voilà pourquoi le roi d'Écosse préférait une *galère* méridionale à ses row-barges. Avec une galère, sa fille serait plus sûre d'échapper aux corsaires, la galère ayant un équipage plus nombreux et étant plus légère. Si le reste de la flotte, les voiliers, étaient surpris par un calme plat, la galère pourrait toujours aller de l'avant et gagner un port ami.

"Pourquoi, maintenant, désirer une galère *espagnole* plutôt qu'une galère *italienne ?* D'abord évidemment, parce que l'Espagne était plus proche ; ensuite parce que les convois génois et vénitiens dits des 'galères de Flandres' ne détachaient jamais aucune de leurs galères au service de l'étranger ; enfin parce que l'équipage combattant était plus nombreux. Au lieu des 25 ou 30 hommes de guerre que comportaient les galères franco-italiennes, en plus des 160 ou 180 rameurs, les Espagnols en embarquaient 60 et plus. Vers 1400, l'équipage normal d'une galère espagnole était de 240 hommes environ, d'une galère française, 210. Dois-je ajouter que les Espagnols étaient bien connus en Écosse où ils allaient chercher les troupes auxiliaires envoyées à Charles VII. ?

"Il ne faut pas cependant attacher à cette épithète ' espagnole ' une portée qu'elle n'a pas, et, pour vous en convaincre, je puis vous dire, monsieur, que la galère proprement dite (je laisse de côté tous ses dérivés infiniment variables : galiotte, galion, galéasse, &c.) est le navire qui a le moins changé depuis les latins et même les Egyptiens jusqu'au XVIIIe siècle. Plût au ciel que les autres voiliers ou bâtiments à rames n'aient pas subi plus de modifications ! Ce serait un jeu de les reconstituer, au lieu que . . . Mais ceci n'est plus de notre sujet.

"Les prototypes des galères portugaises et espagnoles du XIIIe siècle avaient été faits à Lisbonne et à Séville par des Génois, pendant qu'en ce même siècle les ouvriers castillans allaient s'instruire aux chantiers de Gênes. J'ai retrouvé les noms d'un grand nombre de Sévillans dans les archives de Gênes, XIVe siècle. A Lisbonne, durant deux siècles, XVe et XVIe, douze marins et constructeurs génois furent constamment à la solde des rois. De même en France, du XIIIe au XV.e siècle, au Clos des Galées, il y avait deux séries d'ouvriers et maîtres entretenus : des Normands pour les voiliers (barges, nefs, coques), des Italiens, Espagnols ou Provençaux pour les bâtiments à rames (galères, galiottes, lins). De là cette identité de construction, de langue, de technique, pour tout ce qui concerne la marine à rames. En Angleterre aussi, il y eut des constructeurs italiens au XIVe siècle.

"Quant à ce que les Norvégiens du Moyen Age appelaient galées ou galères, il faut entendre par là un dérivé de leurs longues nefs.

"Vous pourriez être tenté, monsieur, de prendre, comme type de la galère, la gravure de Breughel donnée par Jal dans son Glossaire Nautique, article Galère. Gardez vous en. Ce petit bateau n'a que l'avant de la galère. Et encore, au XVe siècle, la galère ne portait guère que deux pièces de canon à la rambade. Mais il n'a pas les deux mats, l' *agilité* et la *subtilité*, comme on disait alors, d'une galère."

II.

A NOTE BY ESPRIT CABART DE VILLERMONT CONCERNING SCARRON AND HIS WIFE.

Copied from the fly-leaf of the "Apologie pour M. Duncan," preserved in the National Library, Paris. Press mark, Td. 86–14.

(*See above, p. 96.*)

" Les notes marginales et manuscrittes de ce livres sont du Sieur de la Ménardière qui estoit médecin de madame la marquise de Sablé, à ses gages et demeurant chez elle et, depuis, lecteur du roy. Ce fut luy qui donna, pour un léger mal, des pillules à feu M. Scarron (mary de madame la marquise de Maintenon) qui luy causèrent une contraction de nerfs qui, d'homme bien fait et très dispost, le rendirent impotent par une contraction de nerfs qui augmenta jusques à sa mort.

" J'ay connu particulièrement madame Scarron avant qu'elle allast aux Indes occidentales. Je l'ay veue depuis à la Martinique chez sa mère chez qui je logeay pendant que notre navire estoit en charge, et, depuis, à St. Christophle, chez le commandeur de Poincy, où nous demeurâmes ensemble pendant deux mois et où elle estoit venue chercher son mary, feu M. d'Aubigné, filz de celuy qui a fait l'histoire d'Aubigné, et le Baron de Fenest et la Confession de Sancy et autres ouvrages.

" J'ay demeuré depuis avec M. et Madame Scarron pendant trois ans . . . à l'hostel de Troyes, rue d'Enfer, où ils furent mariez en 1652 : Madame d'Aubigné sa mère m'ayant envoyé une procuration pour la validité du mariage, m'ayant prié par ses lettres de la mettre en quelque religion en attendant leur mariage projetté, auparavant que sa fille fût en Poitou avec madame la marquise de Neuillan à qui elle estoit et qui logeoit à l'hostel de Troyes avec son frère M. Tiraqueau ; et ce fut là où commencèrent leurs amours, M. Scarron y tenant une portion dont il me loua une partie. Ensuitte de quoy il me prit en pantion avec Lafleur qui me servoit et à qui il fesoit souvent faire des tourtes de frangipane devant luy.

" Ce fut là où il fit, à ma persuasion, le premier volume de son Roman Comique qu'il dédia au Cardinal de Rets, pour lors coadjuteur de Paris, qui venoit souvent passer d'agréables heures avec luy au sortir du Luxembourg, pendant la Fronde. Je luy fournis les quatre nouvelles en espagnol qui sont si agréablement traduittes dans ses deux volumes, aussy bien que les quatre autres qu'il a traduittes et qu'il a données à part. Je luy proposay une nouvelle traduction du Don Quixotte au lieu de la morale de Gassendy à la traduction de laquelle je le trouvay attaché, mais il n'en voulut point tâter accause de la précédente traduction par Oudin et un autre, quoyque pitoyable. Je luy dis qu'il falloit donc qu'il entreprist quelque ouvrage de son chef et de son caractère enjoué, plustost que cette morale de Gassendy trop sérieuse pour luy, et qu'il y meslast des nouvelles dont je luy fournirois les originaux en espagnol qu'il entendoit et dont j'avois quantité. En quoy il imiteroit au moins Don Quixote qui en a donné quatre si jolies dans sa première partie : de sorte que je puis dire que le public m'a, en quelque sorte, l'obligation de cet agréable ouvrage, bien que je n'en soy pas l'auteur, aussy bien que de ses quatre dernières nouvelles imprimées à part.

" J'ay cent jolies lettres qu'il m'a escrittes, que je feray peut estre imprimer quelque jour si sa veufve m'en donne la permission. Il m'en escri[vi]t une entre autres pendant que j'estois à Sedan, qui commence par : ' Que diable faites vous sur les bords de la Meuse,' où il fait l'éloge du maréchal de Fabert et où il dit qu'il ne ressemble pas à ces maréchaux qui n'ont que de l'instinct tout au plus."

III.

A DESCRIPTION OF HATFIELD BY SAMUEL DE SORBIÈRES, 1663.

(See above, p. 180.)

"Je ne vous parleray que de [la maison de campagne] de M. le Comte de Salisbury, à laquelle M. le Comte de Devonshire me mena. Elle est à 18 milles de Londres. Nous y fusmes disner et revinsmes à la ville le même jour, mais ce fut à toute bride que nous allasmes. Achtfields donc est un très beau chasteau que le père de ce seigneur fit bastir dans un grand parc et qu'il acheva dans moins d'un an, lors de sa surintendance. Ce que M. le Comte de Devonshire son gendre me fit remarquer pour m'appendre qu'ailleurs qu'en France les surintendans sçavoient élever bien tost de beaux édifices. Celuy-cy est en une situation fort avantageuse. La veue ne rencontre que des bois et des prairières, des collines et des valons, qui fournissent d'agréables objets à toute sorte de distance. . . . Je n'ay guère vu de plus aimable solitude. Le chasteau est de brique, à plusieurs petites tours couvertes de plomb et d'ardoise. Il a trois basse-cours ; en la première desquelles sont les escuyeries et la mesnagerie. Quand on y arrive par la principalle avenue du costé du parc et lorsque les portes des basse-cours sont ouvertes, on descouvre à travers cette architecture des allées à perte de veue, qui percent jusques à l'autre bout du parc.

"Le Chasteau est merveilleusement gay et le dedans est très magnifique. J'y contay quinze pièces de plein pied fort bien parées, une assez grande galerie et une chapelle. Nous disnasmes dans une sale qui regarde un parterre de gazon accompagné de deux fontaines, avec des espalliers à costé et une balustrade au devant sur laquelle il y a des pots de fleurs et des statues.

"De ce parterre on descend par deux degrez de douze ou quinze marches à un autre au dessons ; et du second à un troisième. De cette terrace, la veue descouvre le grand parterre d'eau. . . . Au delà de ce parterre il y a une prairie où des troupes de daims se promènent ; jusques à ce que le sommet de la colline se hérisse en un bois qui forme l'horison.

"Je ne dois pas oublier une vigne que je vis à la descente de la terrace, ny divers petits bastimens qu'il y a à costé, et dont les uns sont practiquez pour la retraite de plusieurs sortes d'oyseaux, qui demeurent familièrement auprès du monde sans s'effaroucher. Sur quelques éminences, il y a aussi des cabinets en forme de chiosques à la Turque avec une galerie tout à l'entour et eslevez aux plus beaux endroits, pour y aller jouir des différentes veues de ce charmant paysage. Il y a mesme aux lieux où la rivière entre et sort du parterre des pavillons de bois tout ouverts, avec des sièges à l'entour ; d'où l'on voit entrer et sortir avec une eau fort claire, une infinité de poissons, qui semblent venir en foule pour jouir de toutes ces délices ; et qui s'efforcent de quitter leur élément, lors qu'ils s'élancent quelquesfois hors de l'eau, comme pour considérer tout ce que je viens de vous décrire."

COUNT DE BROGLIE'S LETTER CONCERNING THE "HENRIADE" OF VOLTAIRE, 1727.

From the Archives of the French Foreign Office. "Angleterre," vol. ccclviii.

(*See above, p.* 199.)

"A Londres, le 3 Mars, 172⁷.

" Monsieur,—Le S. de Voltaire, que vous m'avez fait l'honneur de me recommander et pour lequel vous m'avez addressé des lettres de recommandation pour les ministres de cette cour, est prest à faire imprimer à Londres, par souscription son poème de la Ligue. Il me sollicite de lui procurer des souscrivants et M. de Walpole s'employe de son côté tout de son mieux pour tâcher de luy en faire avoir le plus grand nombre qu'il sera possible ; je serois très aise de luy faire plaisir, mais comme je n'ay point veu cet ouvrage et que je ne sais point si les additions et soustractions qu'il dit avoir fait à celui qu'il a donné au puplic à Paris, ni les planches gravées qu'il en a fait venir pour l'enrichir seront approuvées de la Cour, je luy ay dit que je ne pouvois m'en mesler qu'autant que vous l'auriez pour agréable. Je crains toujours que des auteurs françois ne veuillent faire un mauvais usage de la liberté qu'ils, ont dans un pays comme celuy-cy d'écrire tout ce qui leur vient dans l'imagination sur la Religion, le Pape, le Gouvernement ou les personnes qui le composent. Ce sont des licences que les poètes particulièrement se croyent toujours en droit de se donner sans s'embarrasser de prophaner ce qu'il y a de plus sacré. Et s'il se trouvoit quelque chose de pareil dans ce poème, je ne voudrois pas être dans le cas d'essuyer le reproche que j'y aurois souscrit et engagé des gens à y souscrire. Je vous supplie très humblement, monsieur, de vouloir bien me mander la conduite que je dois tenir à ce sujet ; je me conformeroy à ce que vous me feres l'honneur de me prescrire.

"J'ay celuy d'être, avec un très sincère et très parfait attache-ment,

"Monsieur,

"Votre très humble et très obéissant serviteur,

"BROGLIE."